Palgrave Studies in (Re)Presenting Gender

Series Editor
Emma Rees, Director, Institute of Gender Studies
University of Chester, Chester, UK

The focus of Palgrave Studies in (Re)Presenting Gender is on gender and representation. The 'arts' in their broadest sense – TV, music, film, dance, and performance – and media re-present (where 'to represent' is taken in its literal sense of 'to present again', or 'to give back') gender globally. How this re-presentation might be understood is core to the series.

In re-presenting gendered bodies, the contributing authors can shift the spotlight to focus on marginalised individuals' negotiations of gender and identity. In this way, minority genders, subcultural genders, and gender inscribed on, in, and by queer bodies, take centre stage. When the 'self' must participate in and interact with the world through the body, how that body's gender is talked about – and side-lined or embraced by hegemonic forces – becomes paramount. These processes of representation – how cultures 'give back' gender to the individual – are at the heart of this series.

More information about this series at
http://www.palgrave.com/gp/series/16541

Niya Pickett Miller · Gheni N. Platenburg

Lizzo's Black, Female, and Fat Resistance

palgrave
macmillan

Niya Pickett Miller
Howard College of Arts and Sciences
Samford University
Birmingham, AL, USA

Gheni N. Platenburg
School of Communication and
Journalism
Auburn University
Auburn, AL, USA

ISSN 2662-9364 ISSN 2662-9372 (electronic)
Palgrave Studies in (Re)Presenting Gender
ISBN 978-3-030-73761-0 ISBN 978-3-030-73762-7 (eBook)
https://doi.org/10.1007/978-3-030-73762-7

Cover illustration: Daniel Ferreira Leites/Alamy Stock Photo

This Palgrave Macmillan imprint is published by the registered company Springer Nature
Switzerland AG
The registered company address is: Gewerbestrasse 11, 6330 Cham, Switzerland

CONTENTS

CHAPTER 1

Introduction

Abstract Lizzo's Black, fat, and female flaunting is posited as a kind of visibility politics because her beingness expands the (typically negative) visual trope of large Black women in American popular culture. Pickett Miller and Platenburg question how Lizzo challenges fatphobia and reconstitutes her identity of fatness into self-empowerment through strategic use of Instagram. They also question if differences between the musician's self-curated, fat-positive narrative and those offered about her in print media outlets exist. Their close-textual analysis intersects with studies of critical race theory, theory of self-presentation, agenda-setting theory, Black feminist thought, fat studies, media studies, and visual rhetoric. Such intersectional potential inserts Black, fat female flaunting into overlapping and disparate scholarly conversations.

Keywords Emancipatory rhetoric · Fat · Flaunting · Visual trope

If I were slimmer, I don't think people would look to me with the same type of like, "Oh wow, she's so brave she's doing this and representing everyone!" [the way they do,] because I'm big—Lizzo, *National Public Radio, 2018*

N. Pickett Miller and G. N. Platenburg, *Lizzo's Black, Female, and Fat Resistance*, Palgrave Studies in (Re)Presenting Gender,
https://doi.org/10.1007/978-3-030-73762-7_1

1

In general, *Black*, *fat*, and *female* are discredited identities in that they are stigmatized. Goffman (1963) describes stigmas as "an attribute that makes a [a stranger] different from others in the category of persons available for him [or her] to be, and of a less desirable kind" (p. 3). One with such an identity is immediately apparent and impossible to hide. However, not all Black, fat females are hiding. Many Black corpulent female bodies "loom large" or flaunt such identities, which has allowed them to shift from negative stigmatization and assuage others' comfort level. Flaunting, then, is a rhetorical act of rearticulating identity. As we see it, a flaunted body wants to be seen and arguably challenges the public gaze through a politics of visibility. Visibility politics "are always a matter of great concern as marginalized and disciplined subjectivities gain representation through mass-mediated texts and, as a result, larger access to a culture's dominant exchange of symbols" (Morris & Sloop, 2006, p. 7). "New" singer-songwriter and musician, Lizzo provides an excellent display of a fat Black female flaunting. She has performed music professionally for some time (as a classically trained flutist), but 2019 ushered in higher levels of celebrity and achievement for the artist that was chronicled via her social media and communicated through various publications. Despite her growing fan base and accolades, Lizzo has not escaped public criticism of her rotund physique, boisterous vocality, and energetic bodily performatives. Yet, she persists in showing herself. As Melissa Harris-Perry (2016) aptly noted—in response to Beyoncé's visual album, *Lemonade*—Black women are now boldly occupying larger spaces wherein they are at least now seen. Unquestionably, Lizzo's ballsy self-presentations continue for us all to see and hear.

In addition to Lizzo's zealous music performances, her public communication—significantly Instagram posts and print media interviews—is provocative. Her words affirm blackness, fatness, and femininity as nonnegotiable aspects of herself, rather than as a temporary state needing to be remedied. Such self-defining rhetoric has garnered Lizzo both positive and negative criticism of her embodiment. Plausibly, Lizzo's recommissioned objectification of her fat Black body is a rhetorical element of surviving public notoriety. No doubt, she may be overwhelmed within the welcomed sphere of her celebrity at times. However, as exhibited by Lizzo, Black fat female flaunting is also a kind of visibility politics and challenge of respectability politics because it expands the (typically damaging) visual trope of large Black women in popular culture in a meaningful way. It is why we have questioned *How does Lizzo challenge fatphobia and reconstitute fat stigmatization into self-empowerment through her strategic use of hyper-embodiment* via *social media? And What are the rhetorical distinctions between Lizzo's self-curated narrative* via *social media and those offered about Lizzo by print media outlets?* We engaged in textual analysis to address these questions—a close critical reading—of Lizzo's Instagram (IG) posts and media articles written about the performer with attention given to her weight.

CLOSE READING AND TEXTUAL ANALYSIS

While the terms textual analysis and close reading are sometimes used interchangeably (Ruiz de Castilla, 2017), others consider close reading as the actual technique used to analyze the text (Tyree et al., 2012). This study embraces the latter definition as its methodological approach. Textual analyses provide researchers with means to gather data about the ways "other people make sense of the world" (McKee, 2003, p. 1) and make "an educated guess at some of the most likely interpretations that might be made of that text" (McKee, 2001, p. 3). Performing a textual analysis requires examining the written discourse and the context in which it is presented, including the text in its entirety, the genre, and the text's relation to the society-at-large (McKee, 2001). Researchers can uncover important themes by carefully reading a selected text (Ruiz de Castilla, 2017; Tyree et al., 2012).

As previously noted, our study engaged in close critical readings of Lizzo's IG posts and selected print media opinion coverage centered on her weight. More specifically, our analysis focused on media coverage and her IG posts made between April and November 2019. During these seven months, the musician experienced critical acclaim and categorical music success. She had a Billboard Hot 100 number-one single for seven weeks (*Truth Hurts*) and received eight Grammy nominations for the following categories: Album of the Year, Record of the Year, Song of the Year, Best Pop Solo Performance, Best R & B Performance, Best traditional R & B Performance, Best New Artist and Best Urban Contemporary Album (Recording Academy, 2020). Even Lizzo's flute (named Sasha) has an Instagram fan account, @sashabefluting, with the verified blue checkmark reserved for public figures and brands. Sasha has inspired flute-themed Halloween costumes and attracts the #flootgang, a nickname for its fans (Cardenas, 2019). Arguably, these achievements and rising popularity made 2019 Lizzo's most successful year to date as an artist. Accordingly, we posit that Lizzo's talent and strategic use of flaunting in her public communication during this time positively shifted attitudes about being Black, fat, and female. Moreover, we contend that Lizzo's use of emancipatory rhetoric are self-defined acts of fat hate resistance and not fat advocacy. In simpler terms, Lizzo accepts fatness as a unique state of *her* being (self-identity) and nothing more.

Most textual and critical analysis primarily lean on Foucauldian thoughts on desire, which is exhibited in the gendered and sexual gaze at Lizzo. The *gaze* in this study deals with how the power relations between the origin of the gaze (e.g., media) and the object of the gaze (e.g., Lizzo) are communicated visually. Jasinski (2001) refers to this type of analysis as a *conceptually oriented* approach toward reading discursive texts. Understanding how Lizzo's complex identity is self-articulated *and* framed in popular media requires "a back and forth tackling movement between text and the concept or concepts that are being investigated simultaneously" (Jasinski, 2001, p. 256). This fluctuating method of lingering on texts (including various reading strategies and textual analysis) allows us as critics to discover varying theoretical perspectives (e.g., fat identity resistance through emancipatory rhetoric, emancipatory rhetoric as acts of visibility politics, media framing, and rejection of politics of respectability) that apply to develop a deeper understanding of Lizzo as text. More about our process of analyzing Lizzo's IG posts and media articles is further explicated in Chapter 2.

INTERSECTIONALITY POTENTIAL

We recognize that this work sits at the intersection of studies, including critical race theory, theory of self-presentation, agenda-setting theory, Black feminist thought, fat studies, media studies, and visual rhetoric. Such potential means there is room to expand this work and, more importantly, insert Black, female flaunting into intersecting and disparate scholarly conversations. While we approach Lizzo as a living text, we do not particularly read her with feminist/womanist thought or theories. We believe it is crucial to understand how Black women are framed in the media. Yes, our discussion of Lizzo is one that intersects with racialized and gendered framing. Therefore, literature and studies of Black feminist thought, and critical race theory have helped us to properly situate Lizzo as text (how can it not?). Nonetheless, our work attempts to understand

Lizzo's self-articulation of race, fatness, and gender as strategic rhetorical acts enacted through the media. In other words, we are interested in mediated communication from and about Lizzo's race and size. This focus on identity articulation and individualized media framing setting through strategic rhetorical acts coincide with our expertise. As visual rhetoric and media scholars, we are distinctly informed and interested in furthering understanding about Black women within communication and media studies. Nonetheless, we hope this study sparks future analyses within and between the intersecting areas of scholarship we noted earlier. There is still much to be explored and discussed regarding Black, fat women in popular culture without question.

Who Is Lizzo?

Melissa Viviane Jefferson is an African American classically trained flutist, singer, rapper, and songwriter. Her performance name, *Lizzo*, "happened in middle school," Lizzo explained. "Me and my friends, we all had this thing where we would just put O on the end of our names. So you know, it was Alexo, it was Nino... So I just went by Lisso" (CBS News, 2020, para. 4). She was raised in Detroit, Michigan, until she was nine years old. Then, she and her family moved to Houston, Texas. As a child, Lizzo took flute lessons and played in her school's marching band. In fifth or sixth grade, a band director's recommendation aligned with her desire to play the flute. "The flute chose me," said Lizzo (Gross, 2019, 13:57). She continued playing through college at the University of Houston, where she earned a music scholarship and studying classical flute. However, Lizzo only completed two years of her studies before dropping out after her beloved father's death, who had always encouraged her to play music.

As an overweight kid in the 1980s, her fat-Black-lady role models were actor/comedians Nell Carter, Marsha Warfield, and Shirley Hemphill (Irby, 2019). Like these women, Lizzo aspired to pursue a performance career. Throughout the years, she was a member of several amateur and semi-professional musical groups. Her journey to stardom was filled with self-discovery, poverty, and periods of homelessness. "It sucked. It was very lonely. It was very hard, and I think that I had risked it all for music," said Lizzo (Gross, 2019, 31:33). One of Lizzo's big breaks came around 2010, after meeting the music icon Prince, who would go on to collaborate with her on musical projects and pave the way for future opportunities in the industry. Lizzo recalled, "when nobody was checking for me, he was checking for young, Black girls and young Black artists" (Gross, 2019, 29:11). Notably, Lizzo attributes her success to a shift in culture. In an interview with TIME, the artist explains:

> There were a lot of things that weren't popular but existed, like body positivity, which at first was a form of protest for fat bodies and Black women and has now become a trendy, commercialized thing. Now I've seen it reach the mainstream. Suddenly I'm mainstream! (Irby, 2019, para. 4)

Cuz I Love You, Lizzo's third and most successful album to date, is evidence of society's culture shift intersecting with Lizzo's burgeoning inner strength. The album is full of one-liners such as: "Bad bitch in the mirror like yeah, I'm in love," from the song *Soulmate*; and "Only exes that I care about are in my fucking chromosomes," from *Like a Girl*. Lizzo screams and sings her identity out loud. The album is emancipatory rhetoric, and society was finally ready for it.

Self-Defining as Fat

While this research exclusively focuses on the mediated communication about and from Lizzo, it is important to note that her rhetorical presence is part of the larger narrative of Black women and body weight in the general public. According to The United States Department of Health and Human Services Office of Minority Health (2020), about 80% of African American women are overweight or obese—making them the demographic with the highest rates of obesity or being overweight compared to other groups in the United States. Additionally, about 56% of Black women over the age of 20 are obese (Centers for Disease Control and Prevention, 2018).

Before moving further into this section's discussion, we must clarify our use of "fat" over any other term in this study. As Fikkan and Rothblum (2012) explain, "it[fat] is descriptive, whereas the term 'overweight' implies an unfavorable comparison to a normative standard and 'obese' is a medical term with its own negative connotations" (p. 576). Moreover, "fat" carries a negative cultural association with physical fitness. "Fitness," a collective term typically prescribed to normalized bodies, is centered on the politics of gender, race, and ability rather than health (Kulbaga & Spencer, 2018). Lizzo identifies as fat and has built a brand upon the traditionally negative epithet. To her, fat is not an insult; it's a fact. In an interview with SELF Magazine, Lizzo recalled an early memory of being called fat, saying, "There was this boy in fifth grade, and he would call me fat ass all the time. He was the most popular guy in school, real cute, a basketball player...Around seventh grade, I was like, 'Yeah, my ass is fat. What's good?'" (Cruel, 2017, para. 1). We appreciate Lizzo's self-defining as fat as authorization to use the term as a disparate identification marker in the same manner that she applies it to herself. As Snider (2018) explains, "self-defining differs from widespread identity-based psychological concepts in the way that it explicitly addresses Black women's resistance to stereotypes. It is considered as a counter-hegemonic knowledge essential for consciousness-raising" (p. 13). The performer has argued that a thinner woman would not be labeled as "brave" for exhibiting the same performativity as she. Lizzo explicates this double standard of acceptance for People magazine by saying, "When people look at my body and be like, 'Oh my God, she's so brave,' it's like, 'No, I'm not.' I'm just fine. I'm just me. I'm just sexy" (Boucher, 2019, para. 3). She echoed similar sentiments in a 2018 NPR interview with reporter Terry Gross. "About ten years ago, I made the decision that I just wanted to be happy with my body, and I just wanted to be happy with who I am and that I would wake up with the same body and it wasn't going to change," Lizzo told Gross. "And that was the beginning of my journey with learning how to love my body, and it most certainly didn't end there, and it didn't apex there. I had to work for many, many years to get to this point." She added, "You have to find that love for yourself deep down inside, underneath all of that questioning and ickiness."

Indubitably, Lizzo's fatness has been marked and disciplined as the antithesis of health and beauty. Celebrity fitness trainer Jillian Micheals—a white lesbian—publicly questioned the celebration of Lizzo's physique during the Twitter morning show, *AM to DM*, saying: "Why are we celebrating her body? Cause it isn't going to be awesome if she gets diabetes" (8:38). Micheals retorted, "I'm just being honest. There's never a moment when I'm like, I'm so glad she's overweight" (AM to DM, 2020, 8:54). Michaels' critique suggested that publicly lauding Lizzo's embodiment of fat confidence (or resistance to fat hate) is simultaneously praising obesity and poor health. The implication is that body positivity and fat advocacy are the same—and they are not.

For the second point of illustration, consider the public condemnation of Lizzo's twerking[1] and risqué attire (dubbed "Assgate") worn to a 2019 Los Angeles Lakers basketball game (Sydneysky G, 2019). The performer wore a black T-shirt dress with a modest front design. However, the back was fashioned with cut-outs that displayed her black thong and fishnet stockings. The public's view of the outfit was further enhanced by the stadium's jumbotron that casted Lizzo twerking during the Laker Girls' performance to her hit song, *Juice*. Critics pointed to the event's family-oriented nature and Lizzo's overall bodily exposure as reasons why her clothing and behavior were inappropriate. However, Lizzo believes no one would have seen the back of her dress until the Laker Girls' expressed excitement for her presence at the game. The dance squad wanted to perform their routine, especially for her, and Lizzo was encouraged to sing and dance along. With gratitude and in the spirit of fun, she did (CBS News This Morning, 2019).

However, the truth is, this was not the first time Lizzo's body has been publicly exposed. She sits nude on the cover of her acclaimed album, *Truth Hurts*. Yet, avoidance of the album cover can be achieved thanks to selective music tastes and simply freedom of choice. Nonetheless, "Assgate" is different. As we have seen time and time again, some people are upset with the space Lizzo occupies. This is especially evidenced with "Assgate," as the way she took up space was so defiant—even if that wasn't her intention. Lizzo's body has become a major topic of discussion only because fat Black bodies are [still] not acceptable in society.

If Lizzo was lighter or thinner, people wouldn't have a problem with this. It wouldn't be a problem because people would find her more visually appealing. They would find her more sexually appealing. But instead, we are seeing people go as far as to say she needs to be tranquilized. This statement is not only fatphobic, but it is also anti-Black. Tranquilizers are largely intended to be used to incapacitate (mostly large and dangerous) animals. To suggest that Lizzo needs to be "put down" is to recapitulate this trope about the 'beastliness' of fat Black people. (Sydneysky G, 2019, para. 11 & 12)

---

[1] Dancing in a sensual way by thrusting or shaking the buttocks and hips while in a squatting or bent-over position.

Fikkan and Rothblum (2012) note that "there is substantial and consistent evidence that women suffer disproportionately from weight bias in a number of domains" (p. 587). This includes educational achievements and a reduction in opportunities for romantic relationships, employment, socio-political status, and favorable media representation. To be frank, it doesn't matter what Lizzo wears because there will always be criticism of her fat body and what it is wearing. Later in this chapter, we describe the biased framing of Black women—regardless of their size.

FEMINIST OR NOT?

"Feminist," as an identity, has not been self-imposed by Lizzo. Nonetheless, her advocacy for female empowerment and body confidence evokes feminist thought. Such feministic tendencies have critics calling into question the authenticity and potentiality of feminism of Lizzo, primarily because of her weight coupled with a provocative display of sexual appeal. Essentially, her body is a site for the contestation feminism, *disputing* beauty, and health. As Weidhase (2015) explains, "this kind of critique becomes particularly problematic when one considers the historical (and *(-)crcled* ongoing) victimization and dehumanization of Black women on the grounds of their perceived hypersexuality" (p. 129). Perhaps Lizzo's "feminist" communicative acts are better suited under the umbrella of hip-hop feminist, which attends to the intersection of self-sexualizing and female agency.

> Although a feminists spectrum may exist, it is inequitable to suggest that one cannot be a 'true' feminist if one presents a sexual performance or image. A sexualized woman can be a feminist. In fact, to take the issue of Black women's hyper-sexuality out of feminism ignores the ways that Black women have been historically presented, misrepresented, and depicted through sexualized images. (LaVoulle & Lewis Ellison, 2018, p. 77)

Feminist or not, Lizzo's proud flaunting of Black female fatness rejects cultural assumptions that fatness is unhealthy, immoral, ugly, or otherwise undesirable. Black women's bodies have been the subject of gaze and focus in many scholarly analyses. As noted, this analysis will not attempt an explicit gendered or fatness critique of Lizzo's Black female body. But we hope womanist, feminist, and fat studies scholars will and continue building scholarship in this area.

Emancipatory Rhetoric and Fat Hate Resistance

As we circumvent Lizzo's feminist embodiment and feminist rhetorical acts, we attend to her emancipatory rhetoric. Such rhetoric is ingrained in undeniable personal truth (Couser, 2002). As Miller (2019) explains, emancipatory rhetoric liberates the rhetor from the [negative] perspectives held by others because it challenges cultural stereotypes and replaces them with more realistic representations. Frustration with biases and discrepancies within hegemonic power structures typically prompts one to enact emancipatory rhetorics. In this instance, fat Black women—who are often miscommunicated about and visually troped in negative ways—focus on this analysis. Specifically, Lizzo's embodiment of Black female fatness is read as text. Lizzo reconstitutes the meaning of fat Black womanhood through her self-articulations of being 100% *that* [fat Black] *bitch*, which extends popular notions of Black beauty and sex appeal. But Lizzo's public persona isn't all Black fat female grandeur. Her album, "Cuz I Love You," divulges deep vulnerability, mostly as she sings about self-love. It's a message born from Lizzo's long journey toward body acceptance (Gross, 2019). Lizzo's public communication about her identity provides meaningful texts to analyze individualized meaning ascribed to Black female fatness as a non-*other*.

Communication and media studies have attended to mediated acts of fat resistance. Parasecoli (2007) offered a "semiotic and media" analysis that established a symbolic connection between food and the Black female booty. Whereas connections between food and the derrière once humiliated Black women, it is now a resistance site. "This symbol for sex and passion has moved from negative connotations to positive, self-affirmative ones. The booty has emerged as a site of resistance to the shame and self-deprecation often imposed by white culture…" (Parasecoli, 2007, p. 111). Increasingly, social resistance to fatphobia is popularized via individualized rhetorics (e.g., social media posts, fashion). Akin to homophobia, Saguy and Ward (2011) explain fatphobia as instances "in which thinner bodies are defined as morally, medically, aesthetically, and sexually desirable, while heavy bodies are vilified" (p. 55). However, body-positive advocates are "reclaiming the term fat, commonly used as an insult, as a neutral or positive descriptor, rejecting the terms obese and overweight as pathologizing normal human variation" (Saguy & Ward, 2011, p. 54).

As noted, Lizzo communicates fatness as an intricate component of her complex identity. For example, in a celebratory Instagram post highlighting her partnership with Urban Decay Cosmetics, she noted, "I love my wide face, high cheekbones, and double chin! I'm a bad bitch in my @urbandecaycostmetics!!!" Through proudly embracing fat identity, one rejects cultural attitudes and claims the right to define the meaning of one's own body and create new cultural meanings and practices around body size (Saguy & Ward, 2011). Fat-pride is widely evidenced in Lizzo's social media posts. She frequently posts IG videos and images of herself partially nude, wearing sexually provocative costumes, and performing sexually suggestive moves—mostly captioned with fat affirming and sexually charged words. More about her posts is argued in-depth in Chapter 2. However, it is appropriate to say that IG is a tool through which Lizzo showcases and self-love for her body. We know that "bodies are texts, therefore, because they are subject to reading. Bodies are, in essence, places where cultural values and ideals are symbolically written" (Edwards & Esposito, 2018, p. 341). More about the cultural values and ideas about Black female bodies are noted in the next section.

MEDIA FRAMING OF BLACK WOMEN

Researchers across disciplines have explored the relationship between body image and the mass media (Coyne et al., 2018; Field et al., 1999; Roberts & Muta, 2017; Ravary et al., 2019; Sheldon & Wiegand, 2019; Silverstein et al., 1986). Communication researchers have also examined this topic (Chen et al., 2012; Edwards & Esposito, 2018; Smith et al., 2013; Zhang et al., 2009). Long-standing negative stereotypes of Black women function as visual tropes for the collective understanding of Black women's existence. Collins (2004) identifies these stereotypes as controlling images. Their intent is to categorize Black women into one of few performance typologies—The Mammie(also spelled Mammy), Jezebel, and Sapphire—that have all been identified deconstructed in twentieth-century communication scholarship. Of these long-standing and negative tropes, Mammie may be the most paradoxical to Lizzo because of her skin tone, physical size, exuberant persona, and jubilant performances. Yet, as we have described, her beingness prompts negative critiques that have been too reminiscent of mammy. Azealia Banks' (a Black female rapper from Harlem, New York) unfounded Instagram post represents this point. Banks had an inveterated reputation for "talking down the success and appearance of others" and decidedly targeted Lizzo for her successful single, "Truth Hurts" (Kaye, 2019, para. 3). In the now-deleted post, Banks retorted:

> Lmao [laughing my ass off] the fact that the public and the media has been keeping this fat girl joke going for so long is honestly peak boredom. The song is not good, nor is the dumpy fat girl spectacle live set she does. Saddest bit is that the girl is legit talented and truly only being allowed to shine so long as she allows herself to be this millennial mammy of sorts. (Rhodes, 2019, para. 3)

Yahoo! Life shared a screengrab of Banks' comments before they were removed from Banks' social media platform (Kaye, 2019). However, this was not the first time that Banks attacked Lizzo. In June 2019, the rapper suggested, "She [Lizzo] knows white America loves itself a fat Black wide-eyed mammy and she's playing directly into it" (Price, 2019, para. 8). Banks' accusatory and loathsome rants illustrate how destructive and long-standing the rhetorical influence of mammy has been. Here, we have a Black woman, Banks, publicly ascribe the mammy trope to another Black woman, Lizzo, as a means of disciplining her for her size and mass appeal.

> Mammy was portrayed as dark-skinned, often pitch black, in a society that regarded Black skin as ugly, tainted. She was obese, sometimes morbidly overweight…The implicit assumption was this: No reasonable white man would choose a fat, elderly Black woman instead of the idealized white woman. The Black mammy was portrayed as lacking all sexual and sensual qualities. The de-eroticism of mammy meant that the white wife—and by extension, the white family, was safe. (The Mammy Caricature, para. 6)

However, jovial fat Black women can and do exude erotic desire and appeal.

> Lizzo's performances and IG posts demonstrate seduction as she routinely oozes sensuality in her lyrics, words, and actions. "Although most Black women would not see themselves as nor aspire to be Mammies, they do closely identify with the image of the strong Black woman" (Beauboeuf-Lafontant, 2003, p. 113). Embedded within this imagery is the idea that Black women can endure anything. They are also resilient and capable of carrying others over the most challenging thresholds—even at the expense

of themselves. "Because the strong Black woman discourse is upheld both within and outside of the Black community, there is very little resonance for any African American woman who acknowledges or desires to speak about her weaknesses, pains, and frustrations" (Beauboeuf-Lafontant, 2003, p. 115). However, Lizzo does publicly communicate about her weaknesses and pain. Her honesty and vulnerability are points of identification between her and her fans. Through the sharing of personal narratives of pain and insecurities, Lizzo becomes less of a celebrity and more of a girlfriend with real-world problems.

Contemporary research of communication, media, and gender (LaVoulle & Lewis Ellison, 2018; Snider, 2018; Weidhase, 2015) has extended the foundational works of theorists like Patricia Hill-Collins, bell hooks, and Kimberlé Crenshaw. These studies point toward new reiterations of controlling images of Black women, which include bad (that) bitches, baby-mamas, and THOTs (that whore/ho over there). These works continue to challenge Black female bodies' visual tropes and prompt more critical thought about the rhetorical power of seeing these bodies within the context of popular culture. With the pervasiveness of technology, the (once traditional Jezebel, Sapphire) stereotypes from television and film have given way to newer tropes such as Black ratchet women and THOTs who mask sexual subjectification as sexual authority and power. Ratchet Black women are often described within popular culture as excessive and hyper-visible (Lundy, 2018). George (2015) distinguishes ratchet as a reproachful label used to situate Black women's behavior as raunchy, unrefined, or ignorant. However, other scholars have denoted ratchetness as behavior that is freedom from forced respectability (Cooper, 2012; Pickens, 2015). THOTs are strategically re-sexualized and re-commodified female bodies that move from a male-judging gaze to a self-policing, narcissistic gaze. THOTs are hypersexual for a purpose, typically social status, and monetary gain. The term is frequently used in reality television programming among Black women about other Black women, and it demonstrates intragender oppression that further demeans Black women collectively (Lundy, 2018). Given the past and current harmful tropes of Black women in media, fatness, a disparate negative marker, only further exacerbates the perception of ratchetness and THOTs for Black women in media.

Historically, society has been overcritical, unappreciative, and unkind to fat, Black women (Gay, 2017; Laymon, 2018; McMillan-Cottom,

2019; Senyonga, 2017; Strings, 2019). These women face misconceptions about their health and physical abilities (Unbothered, 2020). They are viewed as "deadly" and "social dead weight" because of a perceived over willingness to engage in high-risk behaviors that can endanger and overburden themselves and others (Strings, 2015, p. 108). Their bodies are seen as distasteful and censored on social media (Garcia, 2020; Savin, 2020). Just as importantly, they are strongly encouraged to lose weight as a prerequisite for social and romantic acceptance (Gentles-Peart, 2016; Unbothered, 2020; Whitfield, 2018).

Fat Black women are often forced to be their own advocates. In large part, that advocacy has involved rejecting negative mainstream discourse by reframing their stories into more positive counter-narratives. Patterson-Faye (2016) found these strong threads of reclaimed narratives "highlight this group's visibility, proving that they are indeed worthy of (sexual) attention and powerful enough for self-definition" (p. 940). This advocacy also entails discarding the "obesity label" and the use of the Body Mass Index, which are viewed as products of White measures of health and wellness (Cameron et al., 2018). Resistance has also meant publicly calling out offenders and drawing attention to the disparities in fat acceptance across different races.

In July 2020, plus-size model Nyome Nicholas-Williams, who uses the Instagram handle @CurvyNyome, was angered to find that an artistic topless photo of hers was removed from the app because it allegedly violated Instagram's Community Guidelines. Nicholas-Williams (2020a) wrote an open letter to Instagram, further expressing her frustration.

> When Emily Ratajkowski, Kylie Jenner, Playboy, Kim Kardashian and millions of other notable influencers or slim, white celebrities upload near nude pictures of themselves, their pictures are not in violation of Instagram's Community Guidelines; however my pictures (which showed less of my body) were removed and my account threatened with closure... It is abundantly clear that Instagram reproduces the same racial biases that society does. Seeing fat Black bodies as "too much" or unpalatable.

She also created the hashtag campaign #IwantToSeeNyome to draw attention to the alleged body discrimination against Black women on the app.

Following historical patterns of Black women's problems being ignored or taking a back seat to the problems of women of other races, Nicholas-Williams' campaign was soon overshadowed by an "all plus sized bodies" matter petition (Nicholas-Williams (2020b). American playwright Claire Willett (2018) discussed the matter on Twitter:

> There's a disturbingly common thing in fat white girl culture where fat women of color – Black women in particular – are shut out of the conversation about body positivity, media stereotyping, representation, etc., for a host of reasons you may think are well-intentioned. Sometimes it's rooted in the deep divide on TV, in movies and in the media between the Fat White Woman and the Fat Black Woman, who are two completely different shitty one-dimensional stereotypes. The Fat White Woman is a pathetic cat lady. The Fat Black Woman is 'sassy.'

She sarcastically added, "What's funnier than a fat Black lady having the audacity to think of herself as attractive. Lol. How Dare She."

It is common knowledge the entertainment industry has long favored thin women with a European aesthetic over Black women with Afrocentric features, including larger body frames. "For years, it has been a running joke that fat women in the music industry are only supposed to be the background singers to thinner women. They are never supposed to be in front taking lead, they are never supposed to take attention away from someone thinner; never supposed to bring attention to themselves" (SydneySky, 2019, para. 1). Black female and iconic performers like Ma Rainey, Aretha Franklin, Jennifer Holliday, and more recently Queen Latifah, Jennifer Hudson, and Missy Elliott have all faced scrutiny over their weight.

Despite her vocal talent, Grammy-nominated singer Kelly Price believed her weight impacted her growth in the music industry (The Core 94, 2020). In 2013, she even started the process of putting together a reality show, "Too Fat For Fame," to help other performers overcome similar roadblocks (HipHollywood, 2013). In her experience, Price saw it as difficult for larger sized women entertainers to be "viewed as anything other than matronly, gospel singer, house music singer, or opera singer" or to be confident and "believe that you were sexy or that you could compete with the skinny girl" (The Core 94, 2020, 0:58).

Like Lizzo, Tika Simone, a Toronto-based singer, has been vocal in pushing for the body positivity movement for women of color (Bahadur,

2017). "We are everything the world hates," TiKa reportedly wrote in a now inaccessible Instagram post. "Fat. Black. Woman. And yet, we exist. Unapologetically and without shame. F*** you. We love on ourselves" (Bahadur, 2017, para. 2). In the next chapter, we return to our research questions and explore how Lizzo challenges fatphobia and reconstitutes fat stigmatization into self-empowerment through her strategic use of hyper-embodiment via Instagram and curated narratives in print media outlets. First, we will describe the rhetorical influence of IG and explain our reasons for examining Lizzo's activities on the platform. Next, we will cover how we analyzed the post and our findings. Following our discussion of Lizzo's personal communication on IG, we shift to communication about the artist in editorial print media. Similarly, our approach critical toward the texts is detailed, along with our findings.

References

AM to DM. (2020, January 8). *Jillian Michaels on the Keto Diet, Lizzo, and more* [Video]. https://youtu.be/hNtlE2Ln7j8.

Bahadur, N. (2017, October 5). *Singer TiKa is celebrating the existence of fat Black Women self*. https://www.self.com/story/tika-fat-black-women-body-positivity.

Beauboeuf-Lafontant, T. (2003). Strong and large Black Women? Exploring relationships between Deviant Womanhood and Weight. *Gender & Society, 17*(1), 111–121. https://doi.org/10.1177/0891243202238981.

Boucher, A. (2019). Lizzo calls out body positivity double standard when it comes to women: I'm not brave, 'I'm just sexy.' *People Online*. https://people.com/music/lizzo-calls-out-body-positive-double-standard-women.

Cameron, N. O., Muldrow, A. F., & Stefani, W. (2018). The weight of things: Understanding African American women's perceptions of health, body image, and attractiveness. *Qualitative Health Research, 28*(8), 1242–1254. https://doi.org/10.1177/1049732317753588.

Cardena, C. (2019). A love letter to Lizzo: How the Houston-raised musician made a name for herself. *Texas Monthly*. Retrieved from https://www.texasmonthly.com/the-culture/how-lizzo-became-a-star-houston/.

CBS News This Morning. (2019). *Lizzo responds to criticism over revealing Lakers game outfit: "I stay in my own positive bubble."* https://www.cbsnews.com/video/lizzo-responds-to-criticism-over-revealing-lakers-game-outfit-i-stay-in-my-own-positive-bubble/?intcid=CNM-00-10abd1h.

CBS News This Morning. (2020). *How Lizzo went from "band nerd" to this year's most Grammy-nominated artist.* https://www.cbsnews.com/news/

lizzo-on-her-success-how-she-got-her-name-her-depression-after-her-dad-died-and-her-love-of-classical-music/.

Centers for Disease Control and Prevention. (2018). *Health of Black or African American non-Hispanic population.* Retrieved November 2, 2020, from https://www.cdc.gov/nchs/fastats/black-health.htm.

Chen, G., Williams, S., Hendrickson, N., & Chen, L. (2012). Male mammies: A social-comparison perspective on how exaggeratedly overweight media portrayals of Madea, Rasputia, and big momma affect how Black women feel about themselves. *Mass Communication & Society, 15*(1), 115–135. https://doi.org/10.1080/15205436.2011.569682.

Collins, Patricia Hill. (2004). *Black sexual politics.* New York: Routledge.

Cooper, B. (2012, December 31). *(Un)Clutching my mother's pearls, or ratchetness and the residue of respectability* [Blog post]. https://crunkfeministcollective.wordpress.com/2012/12/31/unclutching-mymothers-pearls-or-ratchetness-and-the-residue-of-respectability/.

Cottom, T. M. (2019). *Thick: and other essays.* The New Press.

Couser, G. T. (2002). Signifying bodies: Life writing and disability studies. In S. L. Snyder, B. J. Brueggemann, & R. Garland-Thomson (Eds.), *Disability studies: Enabling the humanities* (pp. 109–117). New York: The Modern Language Association of America.

Coyne, S. M., Liechty, T., Collier, K. M., Sharp, A. D., Davis, E. J., & Kroff, S. L. (2018). The effect of media on body image in pregnant and postpartum women. *Health Communication, 33*(7), 793–799. https://doiorg.spot.lib.auburn.edu/10.1080/10410236.2017.1314853.

Cruel, J. (2017). *Body-positive singer Lizzo doesn't care if you call her fat.* Self. https://www.self.com/story/lizzo-interview.

Edwards, E. B., & Esposito, J. (2018). Reading the black woman's body via instagram fame. *Communication, Culture and Critique, 11*(3), 341–358. https://doi.org/10.1093/ccc/tcy011.

Field, A. E., Cheung, L., Wolf, A. M., Herzog, D. B., Gortmaker, S. L., & Colditz, G. A. (1999). Exposure to the mass media and weight concerns among girls. *Pediatrics, 103*(3), 660.

Fikkan, J. L., & Rothblum, E. D. (2012). Is fat a feminist issue? Exploring the gendered nature of weight bias. *Sex Roles, 66,* 575–592. https://doi.org/10.1007/s11199-011-0022-5.

Garcia, A. (2020, October 28). The Instagram nudity policy is changing to be more inclusive of plus-size bodies. *Glamour.* https://www.glamour.com/story/the-instagram-nudity-policy-is-changing-to-be-more-inclusive-of-plus-size-bodies.

Gay, R. (2017). *Hunger: A memoir of (my) body* (1st edn.). Harper, an imprint of Harper Collins Publishers.

Gentles-Peart, K. (2016). *Romance with voluptuousness: Caribbean women and thick bodies in the United States*. University of Nebraska Press.

George, J. A. (2015). Stereotype and school pushout: Race, gender, and discipline disparities in the context of school discipline disparities. *Arkansas Law Review, 68*(1), 101–129.

Goffman, E. (1963). *Stigma: Notes on the management of a spoiled identity*. New York: Prentice-Hall.

Gross, T. (2019, May 23). Lizzo on feminism, self-love and bringing 'Hallelujah Moments' to stage [Audio podcast episode]. In *Fresh Air*. National Public Radio Online. https://www.npr.org/2019/05/23/725704 911/lizzo-on-feminism-self-love-and-bringing-hallelujah-moments-to-stage.

Harris-Perry, M. (2016, April 26). A call and response with Melissa Harris-Perry: The pain and the power of lemonade. What happens when we take the hopes, dreams, pain, and joy of black girls and women and put them in the center? *Elle*. https://www.elle.com/culture/music/a35903/lemonade-call-and-response/.

HipHollywood. (2013, July 5). *Why Kelly price created new reality TV show 'too fat for fame'* [Video]. https://www.youtube.com/watch?v=6WBJYn7aE28.

Irby, S. (2019). *Lizzo: TIMES's entertainer of the year*. Retrieved from https://time.com/entertainer-of-the-year-2019-lizzo/.

Jasinski, J. (2001). The status of theory and method in rhetorical criticism. *Western Journal of Communication, 65*(3), 249–270.

Kaye, B. (2019). Azealia Banks calls Lizzo "millennial mammy" in unprompted Instagram tirade. *Yahoo! Life*. https://www.yahoo.com/lifestyle/azealia-banks-calls-lizzo-millennial-215020064.html.

Kulbaga, T., & Spencer, L. (2018). Fitness and the feminist first lady: Gender, race, and body in Michelle Obama's let's move! Campaign. *Women and Language, 40*, 1.

LaVoulle, C., & Lewis Ellison, T. (2018). The bad bitch Barbie Craze and Beyoncé African American Women's bodies as commodities in Hip-Hop culture, images, and media. *Taboo: The Journal of Culture and Education, 16*, 2. https://doi.org/10.31390/taboo.16.2.07.

Laymon, K. (2018). *Heavy: An American memoir*. Scribner.

Lundy, A. (2018). Caught between a Thot and a hard place: The politics of Black Female sexuality at the intersection of cinema and reality television. *The Black Scholar, 48*(1), 56–70. https://doi.org/10.1080/00064246.2018.140 2256.

McKee, A. (2001) A beginner's guide to textual analysis. *Metro Magazine*, pp. 138–149.

McKee, A. (2003). *Textual analysis: A beginner's guide*. Sage Publications.

Morris, C. E., & Sloop, J. M. (2006). What lips these lips have kissed: Refiguring the politics of queer public kissing. *Communication and Critical/Cultural Studies, 3*(1), 1–26.

Nicholas-Williams, N. [@curvynyome]. (2020a, August 14). *Post* [Instagram]. https://www.instagram.com/p/CD4JD6GAEdi/?utm_source=ig_embed.

Nicholas-Williams, N. [@curvynyome]. (2020b, September 10). *Post* [Instagram]. https://www.instagram.com/p/CE89AYDAMRy/?utm_source=ig_web_copy_link.

Parasecoli, F. (2007). Bootylicious: Food and the female body in contemporary Black Pop Culture. *Women's Studies Quarterly, 35*(1/2), 110–125. http://www.jstor.org/stable/27649657.

Patterson-Faye, C. J. (2016). 'I like the way you move': Theorizing fat, black and sexy. *Sexualities, 19*(8), 926–944. https://doi.org/10.1177/1363460716640731.

Pickens, T. A. (2015). Shoving aside the politics of respectability: Black women, reality TV, and the ratchet performance. *Women and Performance: a Journal of Feminist Theory, 25*(1), 41–58.

Pickett Miller, N. (2019). "Other" White storytellers: Emancipating Albinism Identity through Personal Narratives. *Communication Quarterly, 67*(2), 123–139.

Price, J. (2019). Azealia banks thinks Lizzo is 'Making a Fool of Herself for a White American Public. *Complex Media*. https://www.complex.com/music/2019/09/azealia-banks-lizzo-making-fool-of-herself-white-american-public.

Ravary, A., Bartz, J. A., & Baldwin, M. W. (2019). Shaping the body politic: Mass media fat-shaming affects implicit anti-fat attitudes. *Personality and Social Psychology Bulletin, 11*, 1580.

Recording Academy Grammy Awards. (2020). *Grammy award results for Lizzo.* https://www.grammy.com/grammys/artists/lizzo.

Rhodes, B. (2019). Azealia Banks savagely attacks Lizzo on Instagram in barrage of name calling. *The Grio*. https://thegrio.com/2019/09/05/azealia-banks-savagely-attacks-lizzo-on-instagram-in-barrage-of-name-calling/.

Roberts, A., & Muta, S. (2017). Representations of female body weight in the media: An update of Playboy magazine from 2000 to 2014. *Body Image, 20*, 16–19. https://doi-org.spot.lib.auburn.edu/10.1016/j.bodyim.2016.08.009.

Ruiz de Castilla, C. (2017). Close reading. In M. Allen (Ed.), *The sage encyclopedia of communication research methods* (Vol. 1, pp. 137–139). Sage. https://www.doi.org/10.4135/9781483381411.n58.

Saguy, A. C., & Ward, A. (2011). Coming out as fat: Rethinking Stigma. *Social Psychology Quarterly, 74*, 53–75.

Savin, J. (2020, August 24). Instagram makes changes to stop censoring plus size Black women. *Yahoo! Sports*. https://sports.yahoo.com/instagram-makes-changes-stop-censoring-162600409.html.

Senyonga, M. (2017). Microaggressions, marginality, and mediation at the intersections: Experiences of Black fat women in academia. *Inter Actions: UCLA Journal of Education & Information Studies, 13*(1), 1–23.

Sheldon, P., & Wiegand, A. (2019). "Am I as pretty and smart as she is?" Competition for attention and social comparison on Instagram. *Carolinas Communication Annual, 35,* 63–75.

Silverstein, B., Perdue, L., Peterson, B., & Kelly, E. (1986). The role of the mass media in promoting a thin standard of bodily attractiveness for women. *Sex Roles, 14*(9–10), 519.

Smith, S., Della, L., Rajack-Talley, T., D'Silva, M., Potter, D., Markowitz, L., Craig, L., Cheatham, K., & Carthan, Q. (2013). Exploring media's impact on African American women's healthy food habits in Kentucky. *Journal of Intercultural Communication Research, 42*(3), 228–251. https://doi.org/10.1080/17475759.2013.823455.

Snider, I. N. (2018). Girl bye: Turning from stereotypes to self-defined Images, a womanist exploration on representation and crooked room theory. *Kaleidoscope: A Graduate Journal of Qualitative Communication, 17,* 11–20.

Strings, S. (2015). Obese Black Women as "social dead weight": Reinventing the "diseased Black Woman." *Signs, 41*(1), 107–130. https://doi-org.spot.lib.auburn.edu/10.1086/681773.

Strings, S. (2019). *Fearing the black body: The racial origins of fat phobia.* New York University Press.

Sydneysky G. (2019). Unraveling the fatphobia behind the criticism of Lizzo. https://wearyourvoicemag.com/unraveling-the-fatphobia-behind-the-criticisms-of-lizzo/.

The Core 94! Radio Station. (2020, April 21). Quarantine Chronicles Ep. 4—Kelly Price part 2 [Video]. YouTube. https://www.youtube.com/watch?v=G4Gi3c0aYOo&t=15s.

Tyree, T. C. M., Byerly, C. M., & Hamilton, K.-A. (2012). Representations of (new) Black masculinity: A news-making case study. *Journalism: Theory, Practice, and Criticism, 13*(4), 467–482. https://doi-org.spot.lib.auburn.edu/10.1177/1464884911421695.

Unbothered [@r29unbothered]. (2020, January 16). Go Off Sis S2 Ep. 11 [post]. Instagram. https://www.instagram.com/tv/B7Y3zXynZlY/?utm_source=ig_web_copy_link.

U.S. Department of Health and Human Services Office of Minority Health. (2020). *Obesity and African Americans.* Retrieved December 18, 2020, from https://minorityhealth.hhs.gov/omh/browse.aspx?lvl=4&lvlid=25.

Weidhase, N. (2015). 'Beyoncé feminism' and the contestation of the black feminist body. *Celebrity Studies, 6*(1), 128–131. https://doi.org/10.1080/193 92397.2015.1005389.

Whitfield, K. (2018, October 12). *Fat, Black women's bodies are under attack. Why did it take a thin White man to get our cries heard?* Rewire News Group. https://rewirenewsgroup.com/article/2018/10/12/fat-black-wom ens-bodies-are-under-attack-why-did-it-take-a-thin-white-man-to-get-our-cries-heard/.

Willett, C. [@clairewillett]. (2018, November 3). [Tweet] https://twitter.com/ clairewillett/status/1058604984311341056.

Zhang, Y., Dixon, T. L., & Conrad, K. (2009). Rap music videos and African American Women's body image: The moderating role of ethnic identity. *Journal of Communication, 59*(2), 262–278. https://doi.org/10.1111/j. 1460-2466.2009.01415.x.

CHAPTER 2

Fat Black Female Flaunting

Abstract Lizzo's self-articulated, fat-positive identity, and bodily flaunting are analyzed through close textual readings of (1) her Instagram (IG) posts and (2) print media features about the artist—all released during the height of her acclaimed mainstream success in 2019. Self-love (body positive and political), advocate, and fat hate resistance/rejection of politics of respectability emerged as three dominant themes in Lizzo's IG posts during this time. Similarly, self-love (body positive), advocate, glorifying unhealthiness, and (unapologetic bad) bitch emerged as dominant themes written about the artist. Overall, the multi-textual framing (e.g., Instagram posts, media coverage) of Lizzo presents a complex, yet seemingly emancipated narrative of one fat Black female experience.

Keywords Advocacy · Instagram · Fat hate · Flaunting · Politics of respectability · Self-define

DOING IT FOR THE "GRAM"

To locate Black Female Fatness themes in Lizzo's public discourse, we turned our attention to her 250+ Instagram (IG) posts made between

N. Pickett Miller and G. N. Platenburg, *Lizzo's Black, Female, and Fat Resistance*, Palgrave Studies in (Re)Presenting Gender, https://doi.org/10.1007/978-3-030-73762-7_2

23

April and November 2019. As previously noted, the musician experienced increased fame and categorical music success during this short period. Therefore, focusing our analysis on her personal communication during the height of her success is tenable. Attention to Lizzo's IG posts is noteworthy for a few reasons. Namely, the platform allows us to see the everydayness of Lizzo's communication. The power of celebrity persuasion resides within that everydayness. Instagram's visual and verbal narratives (arguments) construct the everydayness that allows viewers to perceive celebrities as regular and larger-than-life figures. However, not all narratives function as arguments or advance logical appeals that are formulated in enthymematic ways. But, all narratives, regardless of their strength or merit, persuade us of something (Rodden, 2008). Moreover, Instagram (with its emphasis on visuals) provides diverse texts (e.g., written words, spoken words, images) through which users can create layered messages that audiences can view and experience. It is important to critically examine these (multi-layered) texts about and from Black women to expand understanding of race identity expression and racial difference-making. It is also important to question how diverse contemporary texts work to preserve and rearticulate tropes of Black women—especially fat Black women.

Next, the social media platform is a source of economic opportunity for celebrity (Black) women. "As of June 2018, the social network [Instagram]reported more than one billion monthly active users worldwide, and the social media network's daily active users stood at 500 million" (Tankovska, 2020, para. 1). With more than 120 million active users, the United States is IG's chief market based on audience size (Tankovska, 2020). Moreover, IG's ability to cajole popular culture must be underscored. Many public figures—including Lizzo—use the platform to advocate for socio-political initiatives they care most about. Others utilize the platform to display positive affirmations, endorse brands, and self-promote their activities. Nonetheless, IG's addictive potentiality for both celebrities and general users is compelling. In 2017, Time Magazine designated IG as the "worst social media for mental health" (MacMillan, 2017). While the platform is lauded as a tool for self-expression and self-identity, it is also linked to higher anxiety, depression, bullying, and FOMO—fear of missing out (MacMillan, 2017).

Lizzobeeating, Lizzo's official IG handle, was followed by roughly 6.7 million users—including global celebrities such as Kevin Hart, Justin Timberlake, Ellen DeGeneres, and Rihanna at the time of our analysis.

Also, at the time of this study, her profile picture featured the nude side-body image from Lizzo's "Cuz I Love You" album cover. While it serves as marketing for the album, it is rhetorically a stationary flaunting of fatness, blackness, and femininity. Only posts displaying Lizzo were analyzed, as they most represent associations to her literal identity. Those posts were critiqued using the following code words as filters: *big, fat, juice, That Bitch,* and *Bad Bitch.* These code words were selected based on their frequency of use by Lizzo and about Lizzo (e.g., *Juice* is one of her song titles). The following contextual codes were used to categorize posts thematically: nudity, partial nudity (e.g., baring breast cleavage or buttocks cheeks), sexually suggestive poses or actions (e.g., twerking). These contextual codes were determined based on the frequency of their enactment by Lizzo.

IG posts with nudity, partial nudity, and sexually suggestive poses or actions often featured the "everydayness" of Lizzo's actions. For example, her April 14, 2019 post showcases her twerking in a Jack in The Box fast food restaurant with the following caption: "CAN I HAVE SOME JALAPEÑO POPPERS WITH A SIDE OF DICK?" In another post during the same month, Lizzo twerked on the floor during a pole dance class—a birthday surprise from her friends, she noted. However, the exception to "every day" sexually suggestive posts was mostly promotional of Lizzo's performances and public appearances. Her use of the #asschella to highlight her revered 2019 Coachella performances exemplifies this. In another instance, she posed in scantily clad lingerie to promote her feature in the 2019 provocative stripper-themed film, *Hustlers.* Three themes emerged in our analysis of her posts: self-love, advocate, and fat hate resistance. More about each theme is noted below.

Self-Love

We found that Lizzo affirms her Black, fat, and female identity in posts that featured media coverage (e.g., radio and television interview clips, print media articles) of her. For example, her August 31, 2019 post features a clip of an interview between Lizzo and Entertainment Tonight's (ET) correspondent, Keltie Knight. In the clip, Knight poses the following question: "Besides being '100% that bitch,' what else would a DNA test reveal about Lizzo?" To which Lizzo responds directly and with a straight face, "um, I'm Black." She continues, "I'm 100% Black, 100% everything" (Murphy, 2019, 8:11–8:44). Lizzo's *"that bitch"* appellation acknowledges her body's objectification and diverts it to her benefit. Knight's question includes a nod to Lizzo's lyrics in her lauded anthem, "Truth Hurts." In the song, Lizzo exclaims, "I just took a DNA test, turns out I'm 100% that bitch…Yeah, I got boy problems; that's the human in me. Bling bling, then I solve 'em, that's the goddess in me." Through lyrics, she demonstrates "that Black women can be cognizant of and qualified to challenge their own depictions in popular culture" (LaVoulle & Lewis Ellison, 2018, p. 74). Then, Lizzo continues singing, "You coulda had a bad bitch, non-committal. Help you with your career just a little. You're 'posed to hold me down, but you're holding me back. And that's the sound of me not calling you back." The entire song is Lizzo's declarative statement of self-love.

Through song and text, she explains how being *"that bitch"* permits the admission of vulnerabilities with love, yet the resolve to resist being a victim to her emotions. Lizzo underscores the self-articulation in an October 5, 2019 post that features her belting out the last notes of "Truth Hurts" during a concert performance. She is seen wearing a gold corset and sparkling gold flare-leg pants with the words "that" and "bitch" singularly emblazoned down each leg in bold black letters. Nonetheless, it seems that Lizzo does not always take being *that bitch* too seriously. She dressed as a DNA test for her 2019 Halloween costume and shared a comedic IG post to showcase it. The post features the opening lines of "Truth Hurts," wherein Lizzo sings she just "took a DNA test, turns out I'm 100% that bitch…" (@lizzobeeating, 2019). Dressed in a large box DNA test costume (reminiscent of the 23 and Me home kits), Lizzo gleefully dances with an exaggerated cotton swab. She reveals the box test result by opening it to show her flesh-colored leotard underneath with "100% that bitch" attached in colorful sparkling letters. She captioned the post by noting: "IDK [I don't know] y'all…. this year for Halloween I decided to not wear a costume." The post received more than 2.5 million likes at the time of this study. Using both the music and social media imagery of *"that bitch,"* Lizzo rearticulates bitch to encompass hyper-female empowerment.

In proclaiming to be *"that bitch,"* Lizzo strategically navigates through survival to success while embracing Black female fatness as self-empowerment. As such, Lizzo is 100% *"that bitch."* Through self-articulation and visual representation, she challenges the sexual script for exotic bodies. For example, in "Tempo," Lizzo confesses: "Slow songs, they for skinny hoes. Can't move all of this here to one of those. I'm a thick bitch; I need tempo. Fuck it up to the tempo." Lizzo acknowledges herself as a bitch with these lines but clarifies that she is not an ordinary "*bitch*." Within the chimerical hierarchy of self-proclaimed bitches, Lizzo positions herself as one with an elevated need, requiring more velocity, more speed. Therefore, the authors argue that Lizzo is "*that bitch*" because she is both confident and aware of her own needs. Another iteration of "*that bitch*" in the themes found in the media analysis about Lizzo. More about this is discussed later in this chapter under The Media's Framing of Lizzo section.

Lizzo also asserts self-love for her identities in posts related to high-end fashion. Her May 7, 2019 post is most exemplary of this. In the post, Lizzo is wearing a custom floor-length, flamboyant pink feather coat with a matching headdress designed by Marc Jacobs with the caption: "BLACKITY BLACK BLACK BLACK AND FATTY FAT FAT FASHION AS FUCK." The post captures Lizzo's poignant entry into couture fashion for fat Black women. According to Vogue (2019), the Meta Gala is not only "fashion's biggest night out." But it is a fundraising benefit for the Metropolitan Museum of Art in New York City. It is primarily attended by celebrities, young creatives, and industry paragons. Lizzo seemingly commemorates the moment of occupying space among the fashion elite with her assertive post. It is a poignant acknowledgment and assertion of self-love because she asserts that her discredited identities of blackness, fatness, and femaleness can and do exist within the margins of A-list fashion.

Yet, Lizzo takes care to acknowledge the weight of her blackness at times. On Juneteenth 2019, she wrote: "HAPPY JUNETEENTH YALL (followed by a Black power fist emoji)." She continues, "WE [Black people] FREE (but stay woke cus the shackles are still woven into the constitution & systemic racism will continue to plague us like a social disease until we effectively dismantle the patriarchy & forge a new system that reflects the true face of America)." The post is capped with a smiling face emoji. The visual image that accompanies the text is also telling. In the photograph is Lizzo smiling while holding a red and white decorated cake. The image captures the musician from an aerial view. It shows that she is standing above a table adorned with food—three full boxes of Popeye's chicken, two cakes (like the one she is holding), three bottles of Fanta soda and Minute Maid Juice (all red-colored), watermelon, and a box of chicken flavored crackers.

In response, a follower, @ogma_silvertongue, commented, "I see shackles on that table, it's called nonvegan food." Indubitably, the implication is that anyone eating from that table is enslaved to the food. While we do not know if Lizzo ate from the table or simply posed for a photograph next to it, the post and comments about it demonstrate how Lizzo's association with food is assumed and problematized irrespective of her attempt to offer subjective commentary on the plight of African Americans. To assuage such harsh criticism, Lizzo could avoid posting images of herself eating or existing near food. However, doing so would mean denying the everydayness and necessity of eating, no matter what the food selection may be. In this example, the food represents the kinds of foods eaten at Juneteenth celebrations, making it a reasonable indulgence for the moment. Yet, it is denigrated, and its potential consumer is too. Mitchell and Herring (1998) have argued that Black women may unconsciously participate in their own dehumanization by seeing themselves through a discourse of deviance and as "mules of the world" who are overburdened and burden themselves with too much caring and responsibility for others. Symbolically, we may view some overweight and obese Black women as literally carrying the world's weight on their bodies (Beauboeuf-Lafontant, 2003). Here, we have Lizzo acknowledging the weight of her blackness while being judged for the physical weight she embodies.

Advocate

Without question, Lizzo utilizes IG to flaunt self-love. Nonetheless, she seizes the platform's engagement potential to advocate for social and political causes pertinent to her identities, including mental health awareness, racism, sexism, fat-shaming, and body politics. In a post showcasing her positive mantra exchange with the vast audience at her acclaimed 2019 Glastonbury Festival performance, Lizzo wrote an encouraging directive for the viewer:

Can you do me a HUGE favor?... no matter what you're doing right now... can you take a second and pause? Now...Take 3 deep breaths... 1 ... 2 .... and a super deep breath on 3.... imagine pure love coming into your body and hold it right on your heart. Then say to yourself: "I LOVE YOU. YOU ARE BEAUTIFUL. AND YOU CAN DO ANYTHING."

Repeat as many times as you need. Thank you, I really appreciate it. (@lizzobeeating, 2019, June 30)

In this example, Lizzo coaches the audience through a self-love activity and demonstrates her advocacy for self-care and awareness.

She shows vulnerability in posts advocating for mental health awareness. Her June 21, 2019 post is most representative of this. In the audio-visual-text message, Lizzo speaks and writes about her emotional triggers and coping strategy.

> I learned in the last 24hrs that being emotionally honest can save your life. Reaching out may be hard but as soon as I did it, I was immediately covered in love. I used to think of sadness as a constant with fleeting moments of joy in between…but it's a wave of joy [ocean wave emoji] sadness [ocean wave emoji] joy [ocean wave emoji] sadness and my sadness can be temporary as my joy. I went on live to have a discussion about triggers. My triggers are: rejection and inadequacy. But I love that I'm more emotionally honest lately. I lover that I can use my sadness constructively in real time for gratitude. What triggers your sadness? What do you do when those buttons are pushed? What do you love about yourself in those moments of darkness?

The post has received more than two million likes and 87,000+ responses, indicating the rhetorical power of vulnerable personal narratives shared via IG. Lizzo's post can be likened to an open diary or journal entry, or even an open letter of sorts—all of which have meaningful rhetorical functions. Lizzo's open communication about her emotional triggers offers a glimpse into her unfiltered reality, and her testimony about feelings of isolation, despite her celebrity, functions as written advocacy against the silence of sadness. Lizzo's public presence gives presence (and exigency) to the need for supportive virtual spaces and healthy dialogue about mental health struggles. This kind of presence, as Perelman and Olbrechts-Tyteca (1969) explain, is significant because "it is not enough indeed that a thing should exist for a person to feel its presence. Rather, rhetoric has the ability to enhance the value of and significance of certain elements in a rhetorical situation or landscape" (p. 117). In this instance, the "thing" is sadness. Lizzo's discussion of it via IG demonstrates how the social platform can be a rhetorical tool used to call attention to the negative emotions of having discredited identities and the pressure to be strong despite them.

As we've noted, Lizzo has not identified herself as a feminist. However, she does advocate for female empowerment, especially Black females. "Big Black girls, if you're reading this...you're a cover star. Nothin less. Period Pooh" she stated in a November 2019 post that featured an image of her couture fashion in British Vogue. In another pro-femme post, Lizzo asserted, "If you fight like a girl...cry like a girl...do ya thang run the whole damn world" (October 19, 2020). Moreover, she addressed misogyny by sharing her quote from Love Magazine's feature of her:

> I think women experience misogyny in general all the time, especially internalised micro-misogyny that we are not even aware of. But I think women, or anyone, especially right now, you have to be true to yourself. Back in the Nineties being yourself wasn't an option. You had to fit into a mold or follow a particular pop algorithm to be successful, and I think men could always be themselves, especially white men. But now, being an individual will get you there. It's not the quick way, it takes a while, but it feels better in the end. (@lizzobeeating, 2019, August 12)

Lizzo expresses socio-political advocacy, as well. On August 24, 2019, she shared a screenshot of her Tweet (Twitter post) wherein she declared, "I'm not sure who I'm voting for yet, but it for damn sure isn't [Donald] Trump." At the time of her post, the United States was engulfed in the 2020 presidential campaign season, and Trump was seeking re-election. Nearly a month later, Lizzo used IG to express her disdain for President Trump again. On September 25, 2019, she featured her ass-smacking performance. Lizzo is seen with her back to the audience, bent over while smacking her buttocks with each syllable's pronunciation in the word, impeachment (im-peach-ment). Plausibly, the gesture was reactionary support for the start of (the first) formal impeachment proceedings of Donald J. Trump, the controversial 45th president of the United States—who would later face impeachment proceedings (again) in 2021.

Fat Hate Resistance and Rejection of Politics of Respectability

According to Lizzo, "being fat is normal" (Gardner, 2020, para. 3). However, fat normalcy is not without criticism, and it is undoubtedly a subjugated matter within discussions of desirable female celebrity aesthetics.

Viewed, then, as both unhealthy and unattractive, fat people are widely represented in popular culture as revolting—they are agents of abhorrence and disgust. But if we think about "revolting" in a different way, we can recognize fat as neither simply an aesthetic state nor a medical condition, but a political situation. If we think of revolting in terms of overthrowing authority, rebelling, protesting, and rejecting, then corpulence carries a whole new weight as a subversive cultural practice that calls into question received notions about health, beauty, and nature. (LeBesco, 2004, pp. 1–2)

With LeBesco's (2004) words in mind, it is easier to see that Lizzo masterfully resists fat hate and actively rejects politics of respectability for fat Black women through emancipatory rhetoric. Evelyn Higginbotham (1993) first explained respectability's politics as a specific form of resistance needed for upward mobility. Respectability ideology implicitly restricts Black individuality as a means to silence some aspects of it while highlighting another element for the sole purpose of uplifting Black people collectively.

More importantly, the politics of respectability assumed that certain Black people needed to lose their identities in order to elevate the race in the eyes of dominant society. Ultimately, respectability politics placed parameters around Blackness, confining Black activities to a finite list of appropriate behaviors. Those who chose to live beyond those parameters were often relegated to the margins. (Toliver, 2019, p. 4)

Lizzo's language and flaunting are rhetorical devices used to carry out her emancipation from fatness's discredited identity. Her rearticulated identity is constructed through strategic language (e.g., her song lyrics, interview responses, and IG captions) and through visuals (e.g., IG video and image posts, stage performances, public appearances, and print media images) that position a particular subjectivity for fat people that is compelling and free. Essentially, Lizzo reworks harmful tropes of Black, female fatness so that fat is intelligible and supernatural—Black Girl Magic[1] indeed! Lizzo's communicative behavior has an "attribution of corporeal deviance" that resists cultural rules about what bodies should be or

---

[1] A social media hashtag, social movement, and collective expression coined by CaShawn Thompson (Flake, 2017) used to acknowledge and celebrate the achievements of Black women.

do (Garland-Thomson, 1997). As she noted in the Billboard magazine feature, "I can do anything, you know? You want a polished, choreographed performance? I can give you that. You want to feel like you're in church? I can give you that" (Lopez, 2019). She can, and she does give it all on stage. After all, she has wowed the likes of Beyoncé and Rihanna. Perhaps Lizzo's limitless attitude, boisterous voice, and full-body dancing is a kind of ratchetness that refuses to comply with the respectability of politics, as Cooper (2012) and Pickens (2015) have described. Stallings (2013) has identified Black Ratchet Imagination (BRI) as a reconstructive tool permitting Black people to imagine new worlds and prioritize creativity over rationality. "BRI assumes that Black people who exist within the space of ratchetness redefine what it means to be and exist in a Black body, reconstructing racist notions that restrict Black people to dominant norms" (Toliver, 2019, p. 3).

The Media's Framing of Lizzo

A long-held maxim of media effects is that the media can tell us what to think and what to think about (Cohen, 1963; McCombs et al., 2001). Through the act of producing content and using specific discourse, audio, and visuals, media can play a large role in driving conversations and influencing opinions (Scheufele & Tewksbury, 2007; Weaver 2007; Yioutas & Segvic, 2003). Thus, it stands to reason that media coverage of Black women's bodies can push this topic to the forefront of discussions and set the tone through which opinions are shaped. This idea of tone sits at the heart of this study's inquiry. The images and discourse used to describe a subject can heavily influence audience perceptions and understanding. This concept is known as framing theory. Robert Entman (1993) offered one of the most cited definitions of framing.

> To frame is to select some aspects of a perceived reality and make them more salient in a communicating text, in such a way as to promote a particular problem definition, causal interpretation, moral evaluation and/or treatment recommendation for the item described. (p. 52)

A simple stroll through the grocery store checkout line or scroll through social media sites or online news search engines can reveal examples of media framing of Black women. The headlines and publication cover broadcast messages praising, applauding, scrutinizing, questioning and admonishing everything about Black women from their hair and nails to hygiene and body shapes. These frames paint a picture of Black women, positive or negative, from the writers' points of view. This happens in online entertainment and lifestyle sites like Madame Noire, Media Takeout, Bustle, and Entertainment Tonight (Brockworth, 2019; Page Six Team, 1999; Seemayer, 2015; Uwumarogie, 2016) and magazine television shows (The View, 2019). It even happens through straight news and opinion coverage within traditional magazines and newspapers (Bate, 2020; D'Zurilla, 2017; Fontaine, 2010; Gross, 2019; Kurutz, 2018; Nnadi, 2018; Shropshire, 2011).

While there has been a considerable amount of research on the relationship between media coverage and body weight, much of it focuses on white women with scant attention paid to Black women. Scholar E.-K. Daufin (2020) contends the disparity in fat studies research focusing on Black women is largely because many do not believe Black women deal with weight stigma; thus, there is no reason to research the subject. Daufin observed "virtually no studies or movements look at the intersections of race, gender, and fatness. Instead, studies and media reporting of them often compare weight stigma to racial stigma, as if there were no people of colour living in the crossroads of the two" (p. 162). This imbalance is partly explained by popular media representations of fictional "happy, fat, bossy Black wom[en]"—and some Black women "simultaneously join the chorus that weight stigma does not exist for Black women contrary to their own experiences" (p. 160).

Some of the available research examining the link between media and fat bodies reveals celebrity fat-shaming increases individual opinions about higher weights being bad (Ravary et al., 2019) and even casual "purportedly 'harmless' comments about another's appearance primarily occurring in tabloids and/or blogs" can shape attitudes about fatness (p. 1587). Glenn et al. (2013) found news stories on fatness favored utilizing obesity researchers to tell the story rather than actual obese people. Additionally, Couch et al. (2015) found study participants believed news reports negatively framed obesity as a failure in personal accountability and portrayed higher weight people as "freaks" (p. 8) and "'enemies' of society who were rarely given a voice or identity in such news coverage unless they were seen to be succeeding at weight loss" (p. 5). This supports Bedor and Tajima's (2012) earlier findings that found People magazine typically only published stories on larger, postpartum women after losing the weight. Their larger weight picture could serve as the "before" picture.

Lastly, new digital media such as social media applications, GIFs, and memes offer counter-narratives and increased visibility for fat people (Lupton, 2017). Lizzo herself has spoken about the negative emotional toll that a lack of visibility for fat Black women had on her self-esteem (Tsjeng, 2019). In many ways, Lizzo's recent stardom has contributed to the work of filling this visibility deficit. While this addresses the point of placing Lizzo on the media agenda, however, the way she is framed within that coverage is another matter.

Method

This study situates itself at the point of further examining how the news media frames Lizzo in relation to her positionality as a fat, Black woman in comparison with how Lizzo frames herself on Instagram. To determine media coverage, the researcher pulled a sample of print media opinion stories about Lizzo using Google search. To help ensure search results focused on Lizzo's size, the researcher conducted six independent search queries. The first used just her name. The rest combined "Lizzo" with different keywords typically associated with higher weight people: weight; body positivity, fat, obese, obesity, and plus-size. The researchers also felt the search terms used were broad enough to yield a wide range of commentaries.

As with the IG analysis, the researchers also narrowed down the results by only requesting content published between April 2019 and November 2019. As previously noted, this period was selected because of the tremendous success and increase in celebrity Lizzo experienced. We were interested in capturing specific viewpoints and perspectives related to Lizzo's weight. Therefore, we opted to focus on opinion discourse rather than straight news coverage. The researchers scanned the remaining Google search results for opinionated headlines from well-established news sources to achieve this. In the end, we were left with a sample of 68 opinion pieces. The sample was composed of content from magazines (23), newspapers (20), TV news websites (5), digital-only news websites (10), entertainment/lifestyle websites (10). Of these, 11 came from international media sources, six were student media publications, and nine came from the Black press. The researchers used qualitative analysis software Atlas.ti to obtain necessary frequencies and to organize data thematically. The researcher closely read each article looking to capture buzzwords, context, and each piece's essence. Afterward, she looked for common themes among the findings. The sample of 58 stories reflected the opinions of writers from across the globe, representing various media companies with varying target audiences. With a primary focus on Lizzo's weight, the articles shared commentary on Lizzo's size in relation to everything from fashion and fitness to romance and health. Expectedly, the wide range of authors and subject matter among the articles could yield a smorgasbord of opinions on the woman deemed "the star who defined 2019" (Levine, 2019). Four overarching themes emerged from the articles: self-love, advocate, glorifying unhealthiness, and unapologetic bad bitch. The majority of articles analyzed fell into multiple categories, with nearly all expressing positive sentiments about Lizzo.

Themes

Self-Love

A major part of Lizzo's brand is her push for self-love (Enjoli, 2020; Harvey, 2020; Hurtado, 2020; Lizzo, 2020). Over the past few years, her name has arguably become synonymous with the concept of unconditionally loving oneself. As this study's findings reveal, Lizzo's self-love branding was not overlooked by the media. Nearly all of the media coverage analyzed acknowledged Lizzo as a beacon of self-love demonstrated through body positivity, confidence, transparency, and authenticity. The media observed Lizzo spreading her philosophy of self-appreciation in multiple ways, one of which was her desire to buck non-inclusive beauty standards. For example, Britt Stephens (2019) of Pop Sugar UK presented a collection of what she considered to be 60 of Lizzo's sexiest photos. Another example came from Hello Beautiful, a news and lifestyle website for Black women that prides itself on "providing a space for Black women to explore the subject [of beauty] from the inside out (2020)." A November 22 editorial on the site shared nine sultry images and videos of the voluptuous entertainer happily showing off her breasts and butt.

Moreover, writers also assessed Lizzo's song lyrics as expressions of self-love. In an April 29, 2019, article, CNN journalist Kendall Trammell applauded Lizzo for the love thyself messaging pushed through her music. She pointed to songs like "Coconut Oil" and "Good As Hell" as examples of the entertainer's "self-love mantras that empower a demographic we rarely see celebrated: plus-sized Black women" (para. 4). Margaret Abrams' (2019) piece in London's *Evening Standard* also agreed with Lizzo's lyrics as influential for self-appreciation. Abrams cited lyrics such as "No, I'm not a snack at all, look, baby, I'm the whole damn meal"; "I like chardonnay, get better over time;" and "I woke up in this, I woke up in this - in my skin." In addition to lyrics, other authors framed Lizzo as an archetype for high self-worth because of her visuals. These visuals included self-selected images uploaded to her social media accounts, which is addressed in another part of this study, as well as media shot images.

On November 22, 2019, Buzzfeed staff writer Krista Torres wrote a lighthearted piece about Lizzo sharing pictures of her butt on Instagram. In one picture, Lizzo superimposed her butt on cartoon character Homer Simpson's face. Torres found the picture funny and said she admired the photo's message of body positivity and Lizzo's joking personality. *Women's Health* magazine also delighted in Lizzo's visuals. After Lizzo posted a nude picture of herself laying in a bathtub full of Skittles on Instagram, reporter Emily Shiffer (2019) credited the entertainer with breaking the Internet and being "unapologetically herself" (para. 6).

Some writers took note of Lizzo's signature communication of self-love in the singer's willingness to be transparent and open about her background and her life's ups and downs. Veronica Wells (2019), of Madame Noire, pointed to a prior interview Lizzo gave discussing her ex-boyfriend. Reportedly, Lizzo recalled her then-boyfriend passed along unsolicited feedback from his friends that she needed to lose weight to appear more attractive. After giving it some thought, she eventually realized the entire situation was insulting. "I'm not going to be able to please everyone with my outward appearance," she reportedly said (para. 11). Lizzo also stated, "All that matters is what I think of it. And I had to go so deep inside myself and look in the mirror. Looking in the mirror and accepting what's in the mirror is very, very difficult. And right now, I love it every time I look in the mirror" (para. 11).

College publications also appreciated Lizzo's push for personal acceptance. Whitney France (2019), a staff writer for *The Nicholls Worth*, the independent student news organization of Nicholls State University, was happy that Lizzo took time out of one of her performances to encourage the audience to be their own number one fan. "This is, arguably, something everyone needs to hear," France wrote. "She wants us to know that we should be confident in our own skin; we all deserve to be loved—first and foremost by our own selves" (paras. 4–5). Similarly, *The Hofstra Chronicle* Arts and Entertainment Editor Eleni Kothesakis wrote:

While her music presents an entertaining perspective on self-love, that exact concept is something that many people struggle with in today's society. Many people find self-care and having love and respect for yourself to be selfish acts, but Lizzo embraces them. "Juice" is just one in a long list of Lizzo's songs that promotes the message that self-love is important and shouldn't be stigmatized. (para. 4)

Additionally, Abby Hofstetter (2019), the opinion editor for *Washington Square News*, New York University's independent student newspaper, wrote a touching piece on Lizzo's impact on her life. Hoftstetter revealed her long struggle with body acceptance. Unrelatable fat spokespeople exacerbated the issue, airbrushed and visually manipulated representations of larger sized people in the media and fat people being the butt of jokes. Hofstetter's piece aptly titled "Lizzo, I'm Crying Cuz I Love You" credited the singer with unknowingly helping Hofstetter improve her self-esteem.

Lizzo offers her own honest look at what it's like to live as a fat woman, and the life she presents is full of love from both herself and others. This life had not been offered to fat women before. Lizzo is fat, but she almost never addresses this as either a pro or con—it's stated as fact only when relevant, then left alone...Lizzo loves herself, and she doesn't love herself despite being fat—she loves herself because she has every reason to. Lizzo is weird—she doesn't conform to one genre, let alone the entertainment industry's expectations for a fat woman. She carries a flute in one hand and a platinum single in the other. Her vulnerability lends her power, and her confidence comes unchallenged. (paras. 8–10)

Lastly, writers like Becky Hughes (2019) and Corinne Sullivan (2019) of *Elite Daily* see Lizzo's push for self-love and body positivity in everything she does. Sullivan wrote, "Lizzo is like that friend who forces you to put on a cute outfit and go dancing when all you want to do is cry and reread old texts from your ex" (para. 2). *Elle* magazine's Madison Feller's major takeaway from Lizzo is focusing on your own "wants and desires and, you know, being hot" (para. 1). In summary, Lizzo's efforts to encourage high self-esteem were not only captured by the media; they also commended them. Writers framed Lizzo's self-love messaging as something good, even encouraging the entertainer to keep it going. The ways Lizzo serves as her own best cheerleader resonated with writers in a way that inspired them to share their own stories with the world.

Advocate

Merriam-Webster defines advocacy as "the act or process of supporting a cause or proposal" (Advocacy, 2020). Like self-love, the articles reviewed also largely depicted Lizzo as someone who strongly supports several causes relative to overweight Black women. In Lizzo's case, a large part of her advocacy stems from representing fat Black women in mainstream spaces. Conti (2019), Chavez (2019), and other authors wrote pieces akin to love letters expressing their appreciation to Lizzo for providing voice and visuals for this historically underrepresented demographic in the mainstream gaze. Savannah Weinstock, of *Dig Boston*, was also one of those writers. Weinstock (2019) saw Lizzo's efforts as helping dismantle the invisibility of large people in pop culture representations and wrote, "[A]fabulously fat singer Lizzo was on The Ellen Show, the Tonight Show, the cover of the fashion magazine the Cut, and featured in Playboy all within the last month, each time wearing an equally scandalous yet stylish outfit" (para. 9).

Shakeena Johnson (2019) of *Metro UK* also spoke highly of the famous entertainer. In her August 27 piece, Johnson recalled her struggles with body positivity and the sadness of not seeing many people who looked like her in media coverage.

[Lizzo] makes me proud to be a plus-size Black woman because she has shown me countless times that we deserve to be loved. You can't help but embrace the fact that every time she gets up on stage in a bold and bright figure loving leotard, she owns it. She'll happily bend over and smack her ass while telling you to kiss it because that's how she feels. Her dancers will wear what the world sees and calls 'imperfections' on their sleeves and shows everyone that they got moves, too. Her songs are more than just power anthems. She's continuously reaffirming what she knows about herself and what she wants you to know about yourself, and that's some real role model sh*t. (paras. 11–13)

Meanwhile, an article in Glamour (Schallon, 2019) offered a reminder that Lizzo is blazing new trails in real time. Her article offered first-person narratives from fashion industry employees on their struggles with body acceptance. Kelly Bales, executive director of creative development and video at Condé Nast and former editorial director of allure.com, contributed one of those stories. Bales recalled the time she was tasked with shooting a digital cover of Lizzo for *Allure* magazine. To her surprise, it was extremely difficult to find a designer willing to provide clothes for Lizzo to wear for the shoot despite her popularity. Bales wrote, "That was a wake-up call for me. Like, (Hey, get out of your bubble thinking we've really made true progress, because we have not) (para. 38).

Another noteworthy piece came from Sami Schalk (2019), an associate professor in the Department of Gender & Women's Studies at the University of Wisconsin—Madison. On October 18, Schalk penned a first-person essay for Vox detailing Lizzo's impact on her newly gained sense of liberation as an older, plus-size, Black woman. Two weeks before Lizzo was scheduled to perform in Madison, Wisconsin, Schalk, a huge Lizzo fan, began campaigning to dance on stage with the entertainer. To her surprise, her social media campaign, using the hashtag #twerkwithlizzo, worked.

The college professor wanted nothing more than to dance and shake her behind on stage with Lizzo because she got her chance. Schalk described the experience as follows:

> I get pleasure from listening to Lizzo's music — from her embrace of self-love, body positivity, and individuality as a multi-talented fat Black woman. I also get pleasure from twerking, the act of moving your bigs to shake your butt quickly because it makes me feel good about my body and dancing skills. Pleasure is the way I love and take care of myself. And to publicly love a body that the world says I should be ashamed of is a political act of defiance. (para. 3)

This experience, wrote Schalk, exemplified pleasure activism. The term originally stems from activist, writer, and theorist Adrienne Maree Brown (2019). "Pleasure activism asserts that we all need and deserve pleasure, and that our social structures must reflect this. In this moment, we must prioritize the pleasure of those most impacted by oppression," Brown wrote in her book's introduction (Brown, 2019, "What is Pleasure Activism," para. 1).

Lizzo's sexually liberated attitude and wardrobe also captured DaLyah Jones' (2019) adoration. She deemed Lizzo and rappers Meghan Thee Stallion and Cardi B as leading the current "pleasure politics revolution" (para. 5). "Beyond her talent as a musician, Lizzo's unyielding commitment to being herself is itself a rebellious act against Eurocentric body standards too often imposed on Black women. Lizzo, who's a plus-size woman, allows listeners to cast aside shame and dwell in the splendor of self-love and vulnerability," wrote Jones (para. 12).

While Lizzo is not the first fat, Black woman to gain mainstream popularity, she is among the most recent cohort of women "disrupting the dominant cultural narrative surrounding fatness and the value of fat empowerment, and doing so with massive followings and mainstream attention" (Southard-Ospina, 2019, para. 3). *Evolve Magazine* Trends Columnist, Danielle Richardson (2019) views Lizzo as a role model because she "represents the opportunity to be what I never envisioned myself as, giving me the inspiration to continue on my journey of self-appreciation, one skin-tight dress at a time" (para. 9).

Moreover, Lizzo's reach also spanned across generations. Older and younger writers alike supported Lizzo's position to spread awareness of body acceptance. In a July 13, 2019, column for the major UK publication *The Guardian*, longtime restaurant critic Grace Dent shared her weight story. Born in the 1970s, Dent discussed her personal experiences and societal observations of fat-shaming evolution. She also thanked Lizzo for helping ensure future generations of women would not face the same disappointing struggle. Jennifer Weiner (2019), a middle-aged woman and contributing opinion writer for *The New York Times*, shared similar thoughts.

> If I could go back in time, I would inject Lizzo straight into my 14-year-old veins. I would tell my teenage self that she would grow up and see a woman like [Lizzo] owning the stage and not hiding behind anything. I'd tell her that there would be a thing called social media, and on it she could see ads for plus-size swimsuits being worn by actual plus-size women, posing with thinner models like it was no big deal, like having thick thighs was no different from having red hair. I'd explain how she'd be able to load up her Instagram feed with athletes and models and singers and yoga instructors whose bodies all looked, to some degree, like her own and that all of this would help her walk through the world and feel O.K. and hope that things would get better for her daughters. (para. 7)

Overall, media commentary tells the story of Lizzo as an advocate for the body positive movement and endorses her actions. Writers frame Lizzo as someone who openly discusses issues of representation and erasure as a fat Black woman. The writers endorse Lizzo's push for people to do and wear whatever makes them feel good regardless of a number on the scale or a lack of perceived perfection.

Glorifying Unhealthiness

As prior scholarship suggests, discourse used to describe higher weight people is not usually positive. Contrarily, this study found all but four of the articles framed Lizzo in a positive light and extolled her virtues. The four remaining articles expressed disdain for Lizzo's participation in what one opinion writer called "the politically incorrect obesity epidemic" (Greenbaum-Davis, 2019, para. 1).

Controversial columnist Cory Alexander Haywood offered a particularly scathing viewpoint in the August 26 issue of The Electronic Urban Report, also known as EUR Web. Haywood, who goes by the monikers "The Cranky Conservative" and "Uppity Negro," is known for his no-holds-barred approach to addressing "the dysfunction threatening to rip apart communities of color" and "the numerous excuses created to justify 'negro foolishness'" (Haywood, 2013, para. 1). In the piece titled, "Sisters, There's a Difference Between Being 'Thick' and Being Fat," Haywood admonishes Black women for unabashedly living unhealthy, morbidly obese lives while hiding behind fat acceptance and body positivity mantras.

In part, he blamed the media for "sugarcoating obesity as if it's a new fashion trend, or a badge of courage" (para. 1). While the article does not specifically focus on Lizzo, he does use her as a case in point. In one instance, he shared Lizzo's picture with the caption, "Flaunting all this heft is cute and "courageous" until you gotta get your foot chopped off by a surgeon like Kunta Kinte. There's nothing "sexy" about Type 2 diabetes" (para. 1). Later in the article, he compared Lizzo to rapper Nikki Minaj, who is known for her socially acceptable curves. Haywood wrote:

> Nicki Minaj is an example of what it means to be truly "thick." Granted, she's full of plastic, but it serves her well. There's no comparison between Minaj's physique and singer/rapper Lizzo's. Both women have been called "thick" by the media, but in reality, Lizzo is morbidly obese, while Minaj has attractive, "healthy" curves. See the difference? It's time for us to STOP blurring these lines. (para. 1)

Haywood positioned his viewpoints as tough love and concern for his Black sisters.

Using less harsh discourse, the other three pieces also shed light on a perceived dilemma between the fat acceptance movement and health realities. A short blurb in Media Takeout (Brockworth, 2019) discussed Lizzo having an asthma attack during her Coachella performance. The blurb used the possibly incendiary headline "'Big Girl' Singer Lizzo Has Asthma Attack On Stage" and described the situation as "[Lizzo's] weight nearly got the best of her."

Jack Kirven (2019) also broached the topic in his August 9 column for *Qnotes*, a biweekly lesbian, gay, bisexual, and transgender (LGBT) newspaper based in Charlotte, North Carolina. Kirven supported personal empowerment but questioned whether it had gone too far. He pointed to the music video for Lizzo's song "Tempo" as his breaking point. Kirven wrote:

> Lizzo, and many other fat famous people tend to justify their self-love within the parameters of humor or sassiness. And what is that? It's an inverted fat joke, and how is that actually helpful or healthy? How is it empowering to be huge and knowingly eat crap food in a music video while simultaneously acknowledging to some degree that it's oddly repulsive and needs to be softened with whimsy? (para. 12)

Kirven pinpointed one particular moment of the video that especially bothered him.

> When umpteen huge women in small shorts (so, it's now equal opportunity sexual objectification?) formed a circle around Lizzo and started twerking. Really? Not because these women were celebrating themselves. Not that they want to be attractive. Not that they want to dance and be happy. But because they are feeding into the utterly false narrative that their weight is normal. It is not. "I was born this way!" Bitch, no you weren't! You didn't pop out of your mama weighing as much as two or three babies. Miss me with that nonsense. (paras. 12–14)

In the August 26 issue of *The Spectator*, columnist Daniella Greenbaum-Davis questioned whether what she dubbed as the "Lizzo phenomenon" was simply an "over-correction" to the long-standing media and societal embrace of European-centric standards of beauty and pushes toward unreasonable beauty ideals (para. 4). "It may not be politically correct to say it, but obesity isn't woke. It's a death sentence. Pop culture should stop swinging the sword," Greenbaum-Davis wrote (para. 4).

Negative commentary on Lizzo's weight was overwhelmingly overshadowed by the positive opinions of the remaining coverage. Still, it is important to note the negative frames used to create Lizzo's media narrative. These four writers paint a picture of an obese, not thick, or some other easygoing synonym. This woman has deceived herself and her "army of sycophantic fans" into loving their bodies by any means necessary, even if it means ignoring naysayers and health issues that can lead to death (Greenbaum-Davis, 2019, para. 3).

Unapologetic Bad Bitch

There is no one universal definition for the term "bad bitch." The locution, which reframes the word "bitch" from a negative to a positive, has been used to reference a woman's looks, power, independence, and even willingness to protect and cater to her mate. The top definition on Urban Dictionary defines the term as "a girl who is bold and will do anything for herself and has a great self-confidence" (George, 2019). Lizzo herself has even used the term. In her song "Truth Hurts," she calls herself a "bad bitch" in addition to describing herself as a loyal, helpful independent goddess. In that same song, she rapped what would become one of her most popular phrases "I just took a DNA test, turns out I'm 100% that bitch" (Shafer, 2019) Despite the many nuanced interpretations, it seems a bad bitch can be best understood as a woman who effortlessly commands others' respect based on the total of her positive attributes. As we noted earlier in this chapter's discussion of Lizzo's IG posts, "bad bitches" can and do self-identify as "100% that bitch" as exhibited by Lizzo in her songs and IG posts.

In many ways, this particular theme is a summation of all the other positive frames discussed in this study. Several articles examined used the term "bad bitch" and similar terms of endearment to express their love for Lizzo. Keeping with its site's mission, staff writers at Hello Beautiful (2019) held nothing back when they praised Lizzo in a November 22 editorial for her inspirational confidence and sexiness. The editorial noted lessons learned from the "bad b*tch" included "confidence is sexy, big girls are popping, and you can do what you want with your body if it makes you feel good" and shared nine moments to support their argument (para. 1).

Similarly, in another November editorial, Hello Beautiful also lauded the musical artist for affirming her bad bitch status by slaying the cover of the December 2019 *British Vogue* issue. Buzzfeed reporter Morgan Murrell also reaffirmed Lizzo as "100% that bitch" because of her energetic 2019 VMA performance and great fashion sense (para. 6). Lizzo's confidence and impenitent attitude about her perceived fabulousness made fans out of writers like *Teen Vogue* reporter Bianca Nieves. Nieves (2019) said Lizzo's steadfastness paired with the singer's musicianship, dancing skills, and stylish wardrobe as reasons for her obsession with the entertainer. As a nod to the entertainer, Nieves also shared tips with readers on ways to spruce up their fall wardrobe with items inspired by Lizzo's "bomb style," thus acquiring "100% that bitch" status, too (para. 3).

Furthermore, one writer argued that Lizzo's fabulous icon status protected her from the increasingly common cancel culture that seeks to discard prominent people, including celebrities, who commit offensive acts. CNN freelance writer Glenn Gamboa used the 2009 Internet protest started by fans of singer Ariana Grande, otherwise known as Arianators, as an example of Lizzo's impenetrable cachet. While Gamboa acknowledged that Lizzo's race and physical appearance undoubtedly attracts some enemies, Lizzo's success and work ethic have rendered her "uncancelable."

The primary message of the media analyzed portrays Lizzo as a woman who is successful and enviable. As Kothesakis (2019) put it, "Lizzo is everything but the kitchen sink" (para. 4). Writers saw Lizzo as a bad bitch who continues down her own path regardless of others' unsolicited opinions.

REFERENCES

Abrams, M. (2019, July 26). *Best Lizzo lyrics, leotards and quotes celebrating the singer and flautist. Evening Standard.* https://www.standard.co.uk/insider/celebrity/lizzo-best-looks-quotes-a4120556.html.

Advocacy. (2020). *In Merriam-Webster.* https://www.merriam-webster.com/dictionary/advocacy.

Bate, E. (2020, September 5). *Lizzo said the body positivity movement has been "made acceptable" and is "no longer benefiting" the people who created it. Buzzfeed.* https://www.buzzfeed.com/eleanorbate/lizzo-body-positivity-normativity-vogue-interview.

Beauboeuf-Lafontant, T. (2003). Strong and large Black Women? Exploring relationships between Deviant Womanhood and Weight. *Gender & Society, 17*(1), 111–121. https://doi.org/10.1177/0891243202238981.

Bedor, E., & Tajima, A. (2012). No fat moms! Celebrity mothers' weight-loss narratives in People Magazine. *Journal of Magazine & New Media Research, 13*(2), 1–26.

Brockworth, T. (2019, April 23). '*Big Girl*' *singer Lizzo has asthma attack on stage!!* [Video]. Media Takeout. https://mtonews.com/big-girl-singer-lizzo-has-asthma-attack-on-stage-video.

Brown, A. M. (2019). *Pleasure activism: The politics of feeling good.* AK Press.

Chavez, K. (2019, July 30). *The decade of Lizzo is just getting started.* Marie Claire. https://www.marieclaire.com/celebrity/a28542850/lizzo-abs olut-juice-interview/.

Cohen, B. C. (1963). *The press and foreign policy.* Princeton, NJ: Princeton University Press.

Conti, G. (2019, May 21). *I denied my eating disorder for years. This is why I'm finally talking about it.* Hello Giggles. https://hellogiggles.com/lifestyle/den ied-my-eating-disorder-for-years/.

Cooper, B. (2012, December 31). *(Un)Clutching my mother's pearls, or ratchetness and the residue of respectability* [Blog post]. https://crunkfeministcolle ctive.wordpress.com/2012/12/31/unclutching-mymothers-pearls-or-ratche tness-and-the-residue-of-respectability/.

Couch, D., Thomas, S. L., Lewis, S., Blood, R. W., & Komesaroff, P. (2015). Obese Adults' perceptions of news reporting on obesity: The panopticon and synopticon at Work. *SAGE Open, 5*(4), 1.

Daufin, E. K. (2020). Thick Sistahs and heavy disprivilege: Black women, intersectionality and weight stigma. In M. Friedman, C. Rice, & J. Rinaldi (Eds.), *Thickening fat: Fat bodies, intersectionality, and social justice* (pp. 160–170). Routledge.

D'Zurilla, C. (2017, March 8). Gabourey Sidibe on her dramatic weight loss: 'I did it so I can walk around comfortably in heels'. *Los Angeles Times.* https://www.latimes.com/entertainment/gossip/la-et-mg-gabourey-sidibe-weight-memoir-20170308-story.htm.

Enjoli, A. (2020). *10 ways to practice self-love, according to Lizzo.* Live Kindly. https://www.livekindly.co/waitrose-uk-first-vegan-cheese-fondue/.

Entman, R. M. (1993). Framing: Toward clarification of a fractured paradigm. *Journal of Communication, 43*(4), 51–58. https://doi-org.spot.lib.auburn. edu/10.1111/j.1460-2466.1993.tb01304.x.

Flake, E. (2017, February 12). *As #BlackGirlMagic turns four years old, CaShawn Thompson has a fresh word for all the magical Black girls.* https:// blavity.com/as-blackgirlmagic-turns-four-years-old-cashawnthompson-has-a-fresh-word-for-all-the-magical-black-girls.

Fontaine, S. (2010, April 5). Is "precious" star Gabby Sidibe too fat for a Hollywood career? *NewsOne.* https://newsone.com/478842/is-precious-star-gabby-sidibe-too-fat-for-a-hollywood-career/.

France, W. (2019, September 5). *All the reasons why we love Lizzo.* The Nicholls Worth. https://thenichollsworth.com/7007586/showcase/all-the-reasons-why-we-love-lizzo/.

Gardner, A. (2020). Lizzo wants the world to know being fat is normal. *Glamour.* https://www.glamour.com/story/lizzo-wants-the-world-to-know-being-fat-is-normal.

Garland-Thomson, R. (1997). *Extraordinary bodies: Figuring physical disability in American culture and literature.* New York: Columbia University Press.

George, K. (2019, August 1). *Bad bitch.* Urban Dictionary. https://www.urbandictionary.com/define.php?term=A%20bad%20bitch.

Glenn, N. M., McGannon, K. R., & Spence, J. C. (2013). Exploring media representations of weight-loss surgery. *Qualitative Health Research, 23*(5), 631–644. https://doi-org.spot.lib.auburn.edu/10.1177/1049732312471731.

Greenbaum-Davis, D. (2019, August 26). Lizzo and the politically incorrect obesity epidemic. *The Spectator.* https://spectator.us/lizzo-problem-plus-size-role-models/.

Gross, T. (2019, May 23). Lizzo on feminism, self-love and bringing 'Hallelujah Moments' to stage [Audio podcast episode]. In *Fresh Air.* National Public Radio Online. https://www.npr.org/2019/05/23/725704911/lizzo-on-feminism-self-love-and-bringing-hallelujah-moments-to-stage.

Harvey, O. (2020, December 16). *Lizzo posted a self-love mantra clapping back at her Detox backlash.* Hello Giggles. https://hellogiggles.com/news/lizzo-defended-decision-to-detox/.

Haywood, C. A. (2013, April 23). *The cranky conservative* [Video]. YouTube. https://www.youtube.com/channel/UCMRJ_dU6I4LZipMV_OBkvPQ/about.

Hello Beautiful Staff. (2019, November 22). *9 Times Lizzo reminded us sexiness doesn't come in one size fits all.* Hello Beautiful. https://hellobeautiful.com/playlist/9-times-lizzo-reminded-us-sexiness-doesnt-come-in-one-size-fits-all/item/1.

Higginbotham, E. B. (1993). *Righteous discontent: The women's movement in the Black Baptist church, 1880–1920.* Cambridge, MA: Harvard University Press.

Hofstetter, A. (2019, August 22). Lizzo, I'm crying Cuz I love you. *Washington Square News.* https://nyunews.com/2019/08/22/lizzo-fat-women-acceptability-cultural-transformation/.

Hughes, B. (2019, April 23). *Lizzo is singing the self-care message we all need to hear in 2019.* Parade. https://parade.com/873822/beckyhughes/lizzo-new-album-self-love-body-positivity/.

Hurtado, A. (2020, April 27). *32 Lizzo lyrics about self-love that will get you pumped to celebrate the singer's birthday!* Parade. https://parade.com/944081/alexandra-hurtado/lizzo-lyrics-self-love-quotes/.

Johnson, S. (2019, August 27). *Lizzo makes me proud to be a plus-size Black woman.* Metro, UK. https://metro.co.uk/2019/08/27/lizzo-makes-me-proud-to-be-a-plus-size-black-woman-10639521/.

Jones, D. (2019, July 21) *Megan Thee Stallion, Cardi B and Lizzo are leading a pleasure politics revolution.* NBC News. https://www.nbcnews.com/think/opinion/megan-thee-stallion-cardi-b-lizzo-are-leading-pleasure-politics-ncn a1029961.

Kirven, J. (2019, August 9). Fat is not fab. QNotes. https://goqnotes.com/63555/fat-is-not-fab/.

Kothesakis, E. (2019, September 17). Self-love and a flute: How Lizzo rose to fame. *The Hofstra Chronicle.* https://www.thehofstrachronicle.com/category/arts-and-entertainment/2019/9/16/self-love-and-a-flute-how-lizzo-rose-to-fame.

Kurutz, S. (2018, September 13). Rihanna talks Lingerie, body positivity and her 'battle' with social media. *The New York Times.* https://www.nytimes.com/2018/09/13/fashion/rihanna-fenty-savage-new-york-fashion-week.html.

LaVoulle, C., & Lewis Ellison, T. (2018). The bad bitch Barbie Craze and Beyoncé African American Women's bodies as commodities in Hip-Hop culture, images, and media. *Taboo: The Journal of Culture and Education, 16,* 2. https://doi.org/10.31390/taboo.16.2.07.

LeBesco, K. (2004). *Revolting bodies? The struggle to redefine fat identity.* Amherst and Boston: University of Massachusetts Press.

Levine, N. (2019, December 27). *Why Lizzo was the star who defined 2019.* BBC. https://www.bbc.com/culture/article/20191218-why-lizzo-was-the-star-who-defined-2019.

Lizzo [@lizzobeeating]. (2019, April 1–November 30). *Official Instagram for Lizzo.* https://www.instagram.com/lizzobeeating/.

Lizzo [@Lizzo]. (2020, December 9). *Post* [Official TikTok for Lizzo]. Retrieved from https://www.tiktok.com/@lizzo/video/6904153428281396486?lang=en.

Lopez, J. (2019). Truth Hurts' was a viral hit, but Lizzo's Stardom is no accident. *Billboard.* https://www.billboard.com/articles/news/8530113/lizzo-billboard-cover-story-interview/.

Lupton, D. (2017). Digital media and body weight, shape, and size: An introduction and review. *Fat Studies, 6*(2), 119–134.

MacMillan, A. (2017). Why Instagram is the worst social media for mental health. *Time.* https://time.com/4793331/instagram-social-media-mental-health/.

McCombs, M., Ghanem, S. I., Reese, S. D., Gandy, J. O. H., & Grant, A. E. (2001). The convergence of agenda setting and framing. In *Framing public life: Perspectives on media & our understanding of the social world* (pp. 67–82).

Mitchell, A., & Herring, K. (1998). *What the blues is all about: Black women overcoming stress and depression.* New York: Perigee.

Murphy, D. (2019). *Lizzo opens up about her dating life and getting hit on after the MTV VMAs (Exclusive).* Entertainment Tonight. https://www.etonline.

com/lizzo-opens-up-about-her-dating-life-and-getting-hit-on-after-the-mtv-vmas-exclusive-131356.

Nieves, B. (2019, September 4). How to dress like Lizzo this fall 2019. *Teen Vogue.* https://www.teenvogue.com/story/dress-like-lizzo.

Nnadi, C. (2018, May 3). *Rihanna on body image, turning 30, and staying real— No matter what.* https://www.vogue.com/article/rihanna-vogue-cover-june-issue-2018.

Page Six Team. (1999, November 30). 50 Fat Celebrities. *Page Six.* https://pag esix.com/1999/11/30/50-fat-celebrities/#1.

Perelman, C., & Olbrechts-Tyteca, L. (1969). *The new rhetoric: A treatise on argumentation.* Notre Dame, IN: University of Notre Dame Press.

Pickens, T. A. (2015). Shoving aside the politics of respectability: Black women, reality TV, and the ratchet performance. *Women and Performance: a Journal of Feminist Theory, 25*(1), 41–58.

Ravary, A., Bartz, J. A., & Baldwin, M. W. (2019). Shaping the body politic: Mass media fat-shaming affects implicit anti-fat attitudes. *Personality and Social Psychology Bulletin, 11,* 1580.

Richardson, D. (2019, April 10). What Lizzo means to me as a fat Black Girl. *Evolve Magazine.*https://www.evolvemagazine.online/current/what-lizzo-means-to-me-as-a-fat-black-girl.

Rodden, J. (2008). How do stories convince us? Notes towards a rhetoric of narrative. *College Literature, 35*(1), 148–173.

Stallings, L. H. (2013). Hip hop and the Black ratchet imagination. *Palimpsest: A Journal on Women, Gender, and the Black International, 2*(2), 135–139.

Schalk, S. (2019, October 18). *When I twerked onstage with Lizzo, it was an act of political defiance.* Vox. https://www.vox.com/first-person/2019/10/18/20920615/twerking-with-lizzo.

Schallon, L. (2019, August 26). The fashion industry has a plus-size problem. These women want to fix it. *Glamour.* https://www.glamour.com/story/what-its-like-to-be-plus-size-and-work-in-fashion.

Scheufele, D. A., & Tewksbury, D. (2007). Framing, agenda setting, and priming: The evolution of three media effects models. *Journal of Communication, 57*(1), 9–20. https://doi-org.spot.lib.auburn.edu/10.1111/j.0021-9916.2007.00326.x.

Seemayer, Z. (2015, July 29). *Raven-Symone says she was fat-shamed as a 7-year-old.* Entertainment Tonight. https://www.etonline.com/news/168972_raven_symone_says_she_was_fat_shamed_as_a_7_year_old.

Shafer, E. (2019, June 26). *Here are the lyrics to Lizzo's 'truth hurts'.* Billboard. https://www.billboard.com/articles/news/lyrics/8517815/lizzo-truth-hurts-lyrics.

Shiffer, E. (2019, October 28). *Lizzo just posted a nude Instagram lying in a skittles-filled bathtub, and it's everything.* Women's Health. https://www.wom enshealthmag.com/life/a29610302/lizzo-nude-instagram-nsfw-bathtub-ski ttles/.

Shropshire, T. (2011, May 11). *Jill Scott loses 50 pounds, but does she look better? Rolling out.* https://rollingout.com/2011/05/12/jill-scott-loses-50-pounds-but-does-she-look-better/.

Southard-Ospina, M. (2019, July 3). *Why Miley Cyrus' 'mother's daughter' video matters in our fat-shaming society.* Bustle. https://www.bustle.com/p/why-miley-cyrus-mothers-daughter-video-matters-in-our-fat-shaming-culture-18168565.

Stephens, B. (2019, August 23). *Blame it on her juice: Over 60 of Lizzo's sexiest photos.* Pop Sugar UK. https://www.popsugar.co.uk/celebrity/Sexy-Lizzo-Pictures-46537803.

Sullivan, C. (2019, September 24). Lizzo's song lyrics about love will make you feel 100% that b*tch. *Elite Daily.* https://www.elitedaily.com/p/lizzos-song-lyrics-about-love-will-make-you-feel-100-that-btch-18792100.

Tankovska, H. (2020). *Instagram - statistics & facts.* Retrieved from https://www.statista.com/topics/1882/instagram/.

The View. (2019, August 1). Jerry O'Connell talks Mariah Carey and 'real housewives' [Video].YouTube. https://youtu.be/iiAavFGPdpE.

Toliver, S. R. (2019). Breaking Binaries: #BlackGirlMagic and the Black Ratchet imagination. *Journal of Language and Literacy Education, 15,* 1.

Tsjeng, Z. (2019, November 9). Lizzo: "I'm not trying to sell you me. I'm trying to sell you, you". *Vogue UK.* https://www.vogue.co.uk/news/article/lizzo-british-vogue-interview.

Uwumarogie, V. (2016, December 1). Kelly Price shows off new slim, trimmed figure. *MadameNoire.* https://madamenoire.com/727909/kelly-price-weight-loss/.

Vogue (2019). Met gala 2019 Red Carpet: See all the celebrity dresses, outfits, and looks here. https://www.vogue.com/slideshow/met-gala-2019-red-carpet-livecelebrity-fashion.

Weaver, D. H. (2007). Thoughts on agenda setting, framing, and priming. *Journal of Communication, 57*(1), 142–147. https://doi-org.spot.lib.auburn.edu/10.1111/j.1460-2466.2006.00333.x.

Weiner, J. (2019, August 16). The abrupt end of my big girl summer. *The New York Times.* https://www.nytimes.com/2019/08/16/opinion/lizzo-kelly-mcgillis.html.

Weinstock, S. (2019, April 3). Fat People Fuck Too. *DigBoston.* https://digboston.com/fat-people-fuck-too/.

Wells, V. (2019, April 5). Lizzo recounts a boyfriend telling her body needed work & getting to self-acceptance. *MadameNoire.* https://madamenoire.com/1068194/lizzo-boyfriend-body-shaming/.

Yioutas, J., & Segvic, I. (2003). Revisiting the Clinton/Lewinsky scandal: The convergence of agenda setting and framing. *Journalism & Mass Communication Quarterly, 3,* 567.

CHAPTER 3

So What, It's Lizzo?

Abstract Via Instagram and within print media, strategic narratives help to situate Lizzo as powerful, venerable, yet vulnerable, and forgiving. Lizzo and majority of print media present a "real" woman who happens to be fat and Black—but, more importantly, happy. This, of course, signals a slow, positive shift from outdated tropes of fatness to more modern symbols of bodily inclusion. Nonetheless, Black women are still reduced to negative media tropes. However, technological advancements (e.g., social media) have allowed Black women to speak more publicly, and unfiltered about their complex identities and experiences than ever before. This study underscores the significance and value of studying (Black) popular culture and inserting it into interdisciplinary scholarly discussions of race, gender, and otherness.

Keywords Black · Critical thinking · Popular culture

This analysis sought to understand how Lizzo challenges fatphobia and reconstitutes fat stigmatization into self-empowerment through her strategic use of hyper-embodiment via social media. Additionally, we wanted to understand the rhetorical distinctions between Lizzo's self-curated narrative via Instagram and those offered about Lizzo by print

© The Author(s), under exclusive license to Springer Nature   51
Switzerland AG 2021
N. Pickett Miller and G. N. Platenburg, *Lizzo's Black, Female, and Fat
Resistance*, Palgrave Studies in (Re)Presenting Gender,
https://doi.org/10.1007/978-3-030-73762-7_3

media outlets. Our close critical reading of layered visual imagery (e.g., Instagram posts) and public communication (e.g., print media coverage) about Lizzo presents a multi-dimensional narrative of one fat Black female experience. Although we cannot widely apply our findings to every instance of fat, Black women representation, there are meaningful implications about the communication and framing of this marginal group that can be drawn.

We found no significant differences in the communication from Lizzo in IG posts or within print media interviews. Lizzo expressed self-love, engaged in social advocacy by acknowledging physiological, psychological, and social struggles. She also expressed her political agency at times. All the while, Lizzo called (positive) attention to the diversity of Black women's bodies and welcomed her body's public gaze. In doing so, she challenged critical notions of her bodily existence as merely being racialized, fat, sexually suggestive, seductive, and demure. Via Instagram and within print media, Lizzo's embodiment situates her body as powerful, active, and forgiving because Black women themselves are indeed all of these things.

Not surprisingly, Lizzo's Instagram engagement is entertaining. Her personality shines through the videos, photographs, and captions for each post. Moreover, there is an absolute sincerity that encourages followers to identify with her. Thematically, her posts are categorized as being related to self-love, social and political advocacy, and fat hate resistance/challenging respectability politics. Rhetorically, Lizzo demonstrates an emancipatory identity of fatness via IG. Within this rhetoric, she does not shy away from speaking or typing the word fat in relation to herself. She does not hide or retreat from criticism of her form. Instead, we are offered unobscured views of her full body—curves, rolls, and all. As a result, there is more (virtual and physical) space for Black women to define their existence in nuanced ways.

Media coverage of Lizzo was overwhelmingly positive. Compared to historical representations of Black women period, let alone fat Black women, these results are surprising yet welcomed. Countless studies speak to the limited visibility of fat, Black women in the media, the denigrating language used to describe them, and the stereotypical tropes used to make them more palatable to mainstream audiences. Yet, the media investigated in this study told a different story. Across 54 of 58 articles, there was a consistent message of support and love for Lizzo and her platform. There were no significant differences in this backing between domestic and international publications or Black and mainstream, otherwise known as the status quo white establishment media, presses. This largely sends the message that Lizzo was recognized and celebrated in communities around the globe for proudly taking up space and showing up in the world the way she does. Still, it is important to keep in mind the totality of what the media coverage says. Lizzo is not loved by all. Additionally, it is important to acknowledge that while the researchers aimed to gather a representative sample, the articles included for observation were gathered via Google. Google's algorithms could have possibly excluded additional publications with different viewpoints.

While the idea of media rooting for basic concepts like taking pride in oneself and accepting people for who they are and whatever they look like do not seem like radical ideas, the fact that they are being applied to fat, Black women make this observation extraordinary. Perhaps this indicates a changing tide from an outdated older media narrative of exclusion and derogation of this demographic to a more modern story of inclusion and acceptance. The change is likely fueled by better equality education, more fat, Black women working in media spaces than ever before, and even Lizzo's forthright personality, forcing the media to follow her lead. This study comes at a unique time in our societal timeline. There is a body acceptance revolution underway, and we are all observing and capturing it in real time (Moulton, 2019). The slow-burning yet steady body positivity movement is gaining a renewed traction thanks to women willing to cast other people's negative opinions to the side and be themselves, whatever that looks like. It is pleasure activism at work. For many big girls, this means the freedom to exist without judgment and "reclaim our whole, happy and satisfiable selves from the impacts, delusions and limitations of oppression and/or supremacy" (Brown, 2019, "What is Pleasure Activism," para. 1). Taking a line from Lizzo, Becky Hughes, an editor at *Parade*, described Lizzo's overall messages about self-care as "good as hell" (para. 9).

Whether intentionally or unintentionally, Lizzo has become an advocate for this cause. This was even the topic of a recent panel discussion with representatives from For Harriet, an online community for women of African ancestry. Panelist Dr. Joy Cox offered her thoughts on why Lizzo attracts so much attention. In addition to Lizzo's size and race, Cox postulated that it was also her overall presentation.

Lizzo is not what society would typically think a fat, Black woman should be. She's loud, I don't mean that in a negative way. I think just she lives out loud. She does what she wants how she wants to do it. And when you have an identity or identities that have been stigmatized I think that stereotypes hit you a lot harder and so she is constantly being critiqued and looked at as a representation of a whole and judged on that matter by society or the standards that society puts in place for people who look like Lizzo. They say how she should behave and every time she rebels against that everybody is on her like a hawk. (For Harriet, 2020, 14:54)

While she is OK with being an activist, Lizzo has expressed a desire to be known for her legacy to extend beyond her size and race. During an October 2020 interview with television host David Letterman, Lizzo further explained her position. "I'm sick of being an activist just because I'm fat and Black. I want to be an activist because I'm intelligent, because I care about issues, because my music is good, because I want to help the world" (Lizzo, 2020).

Again, with the media support, CNN's Lisa Respers-France offered a cosigning opinion. "By hailing Lizzo as a body trailblazer, we are giving more weight to who she represents than how she represents. It's ok for us to love Lizzo for being a visibly larger woman dancing, singing and rapping on stage, as long as we recognize that it's her talent that got her there" (Respers-France, 2019, paras. 31–32).

Lizzo shows up in the world, large and in charge. This is evident in her Instagram posts, and it is endorsed by most opinion writers and their commentary. There is not much difference in comparing Lizzo's personal narrative to the one created by the media. Both paint a picture of a woman who happens to be fat and Black but, more importantly, happy. The dual yet similar narratives portray her as relatable, fearless, confident, and unbothered by the backlash. She does, wears, dates, and says what she wants. Lizzo is a woman who celebrates herself and is celebrated by others, including the media. This is a win for Lizzo, a win for media inclusion, and anybody else who just wants to feel good as hell.

IMPLICATIONS

Conversations about the increased prevalence of large and curvy Black females and their popularity are happening in the public sphere; contemporary critical analyses of such bodies' framing must keep up Black women are still reduced to negative media tropes. However, technological advancements (e.g., social media) have allowed Black women to speak more intimately, more publicly, and more unfiltered about their complex identities and experiences than ever before. This study contributes to the critical discussion of Black, female fatness tropes, and Black women's bodies in popular culture. As a result, we can better understand how Black female agency works, particularly with Lizzo. She has moved through the margins and claimed centered space (e.g., fashion), resisted fixed and discredited identity stereotypes (e.g., fat, ugly), subverted language (e.g., bitch versus 100% *that bitch*), and created economic opportunities for herself in a world (finally) working through its issues with fat, Black women.

PEDAGOGICAL CONSIDERATION

The study of popular culture is an important element of academic inquiry. Media studies, visual culture, and rhetoric scholars have certainly led the research on this front. Once dismissed as just entertainment, popular culture and popular culture icons (like Lizzo) are now supported as a societal reflection and influencer of cultural values and ideals. Moreover, the importance of popular culture is only increasing with the advancement of communication technology. Pointedly, social media is broadening our media consumption and the meaning of what popular culture is. Now, public figures, celebrities, and everyday individuals use platforms like IG to create content and visual material that can become popularized immediately. However, some academics may still question popular culture's relevancy and approach studies of it with hesitancy. Thus, we want to substantiate the value of studying popular culture in the manner that we have approached it in this study.

Our immediate goal for this analysis was to explore the research questions we posed in chapter one: *How does Lizzo challenge fatphobia and reconstitute fat stigmatization into self-empowerment through her strategic use of hyper-embodiment* via *social media? And What are the rhetorical distinctions between Lizzo's self-curated narrative* via *social media and those offered about Lizzo by print media outlets?* These questions were the result of our critical thinking about Lizzo and her influence. Honestly, we *wanted* to engage in critical thought about Black material culture created by a Black woman and about a Black woman because we *are* Black women scholars. We know that Black material culture is valuable and alluring, yet it is under-examined outside of Afro-theme, race, and gender studies. For us, inserting Lizzo into critical discussions of media, communication of otherness(fatness) was like ripe intersectional fruit needing to be picked and shared; because arguably all media is based on tropes, reinforces dominant social meanings, and prevailing ideologies. Furthermore, social media creates the illusion of a false intimacy between spectator and subject through its depiction of everyday tasks and direct conversations. So, what can these truisms tell us about dominant American social ideologies around Black, fat females in the 2020s?

We believe the answer to this question undergirds the value of studying popular culture, especially marginalized popular culture. "It [popular culture] is worthwhile to study the facets of the media and consider whether they represent a passing trend or a lingering message" (Vega & Miller, para. 6 and 7). Then, we can continue the work of decentering power structures perpetuate harmful tropes of marginalized groups. However, even if your goal excludes doing power resistance work. We believe this study is still useful to professors teaching courses related to race, media, gender/sexuality, and culture for a few reasons. First, educators can use this work to help students to understand that popular culture is political. Audiences often construct and understand their identities in response to the popular culture they consume. These constructed identities then influence their personal political choices and ideological preferences. This is sufficient to say that cultural and political events can be holistically understood when popular culture surrounding those moments is considered. In the case of this study, Lizzo—a Black, fat female— is wildly popular. She has occupied a portion of pervasive media. To study iconic figures like her is analogous to archeologists digging up fossils. Lizzo is an artifact of culture at the moment. Her artistic and personal communication helps to contextualize the hierarchical spaces in which she operates within. Thinking critically about the symbolic nature of Lizzo could be impactful in cultural learning. Understanding how Lizzo is politicized and for what purposes is functionally similar to reading written works of the past to understand issues surrounding all the -*isms* (e.g., racism, sexism) of a particular time. Notwithstanding, the fact that these issues are not trivial—they make up the fabric of what it means to be marginalized. However, utilizing a recent figure like Lizzo can make such inquiry more engaging and critical theories transferable for students.

Second, educators can use this work to demonstrate that popular culture is dynamic. That is, popular culture constantly fluctuates between marginality to widespread acceptance. Artifacts are here today and gone tomorrow. Through the exploration of such ebbing and flowing, we have come to understand complex concepts like artistic resistance and identity formation. Critically thinking about music trends, fashion trends, and social media trends all underscore popular culture's dynamism. Moreover, the dynamic nature of popular culture allows professors to choose current figures (like Lizzo) and artifacts that match the present trend while maintaining the integrity of the intellectual discovery of knowledge.

Third, educators can apply popular culture as an insertion of cultural diversity into coursework and discussions. Popular culture artifacts provide a means to expose learners to cultural differences in religion, race, ethnicity, gender, and sexuality. With continued pushes for social justice and equality and across all aspects of society, topics of diversity remain essential to make progress. The value of popular culture in scholarly conversations desiring diversity is its ability to use familiar music, TV shows, movies, and more—often created by minorities and marginalize others—to reflect what is happening in our world. Popular culture provides a point of reference to extract examples from and point complex ideas to. In this way, popular culture is a viable inroads to valuable dialogue, critical thinking, and more inclusive education.

On a final note, we have pushed for critical thinking more than once, without acknowledging its complexity. Van Gelder (2005) has challenged college educators to bolster critical thinking among students because it does not come naturally to humans. Instead, we are more likely to gravitate toward easily processed narratives with familiar patterns to understand things. As academics and teachers, we must motivate students beyond their thinking comfort zones. This can be achieved when we give students various opportunities to practice critical thinking. Many college professors will teach a course on theory or teach a theoretical framework and assume that students will automatically become better critical thinkers only from imitating the content they read. Yes, exposure to content is important. But we must also help students transfer their understanding of theory to new and disparate scenarios, especially those they can relate to. Through this work, we have demonstrated how established theories of communication and media studies (e.g., emancipatory rhetoric, narrative theory, politics of respectability, media framing) can be applied to modern texts (like Lizzo). We hope this work finds its way into cultural classrooms. The benefits of doing so include helping students apply a specialist vocabulary to culturally trending texts and topics, building confidence in discerning ideas and articulating them publicly, understanding how to challenge biases with well-supported counterarguments, and cultivating an appreciation for diverse perspectives.

References

Brown, A. M. (2019). *Pleasure activism: The politics of feeling good.* AK Press.

For Harriet. (2020, December 19). Yes, you're fatphobic. w/ Dr. Joy Cox and @AmaPoundcake [video]. For Harriet. YouTube. https://www.youtube.com/watch?v=R68B6QmXevY&feature=youtu.be.

Lizzo [@Lizzo]. (2020, December 9). *Post* [Official TikTok for Lizzo]. https://www.tiktok.com/@lizzo/video/6904153428281396486?lang=en.

Moulton, N. (2019, July 17). Why it's time for big beauty brands to embrace body positivity. *Vogue Australia.* https://www.vogue.com.au/beauty/news/why-its-time-for-big-beauty-brands-to-embrace-body-positivity/image-gallery/fcdf81f04120e099616b323a2012871e.

Respers-France, L. (2019, July 31). *Lizzo and the dichotomy of big girl praise.* CNN. https://www.cnn.com/2019/07/31/entertainment/lizzo-plus-size-analysis/index.html.

Van Gelder, T. (2005). Teaching critical thinking: Some lessons from cognitive science. *College Teaching, 53*(1), 41–46.

References

Abraham, Y. (2019, November 20). In an age of Photoshop, it's what is real that counts—Especially about our standard of beauty. *Boston Globe*. https://www.bostonglobe.com/metro/2019/11/20/let-get-real/gdxnhjAGZsrVcQkc7V9UJO/story.html.

Abrams, M. (2019, July 26). *Best Lizzo lyrics, leotards and quotes celebrating the singer and flautist*. *Evening Standard*. https://www.standard.co.uk/insider/celebrity/lizzo-best-looks-quotes-a4120556.html.

Advocacy. (2020). In *Merriam-Webster*. https://www.merriam-webster.com/dictionary/advocacy.

AM to DM. (2020, January 8). *Jillian Michaels on the Keto Diet, Lizzo, and more* [Video]. https://youtu.be/hNtIE2Ln7j8.

Bahadur, N. (2017, October 5). *Singer TiKa is celebrating the existence of fat Black Women self*. https://www.self.com/story/tika-fat-black-women-body-positivity.

Bate, E. (2020, September 5). *Lizzo said the body positivity movement has been "made acceptable" and is "no longer benefiting" the people who created it*. Buzzfeed. https://www.buzzfeed.com/eleanorbate/lizzo-body-positivity-normativity-vogue-interview.

Beauboeuf-Lafontant, T. (2003). Strong and large Black Women? Exploring relationships between Deviant Womanhood and Weight. *Gender & Society, 17*(1), 111–121. https://doi.org/10.1177/0891243202238981.

Bedor, E., & Tajima, A. (2012). No fat moms! Celebrity mothers' weight-loss narratives in People Magazine. *Journal of Magazine & New Media Research, 13*(2), 1–26.

N. Pickett Miller and G. N. Platenburg, *Lizzo's Black, Female, and Fat Resistance*, Palgrave Studies in (Re)Presenting Gender, https://doi.org/10.1007/978-3-030-73762-7

Boucher, A. (2019). Lizzo calls out body positivity double standard when it comes to women: I'm not brave, 'I'm just sexy.' *People Online*. https://peo ple.com/music/lizzo-calls-out-body-positive-double-standard-women.

Brockworth, T. (2019, April 23). *'Big Girl' singer Lizzo has asthma attack on stage!!* [Video]. Media Takeout. https://mtonews.com/big-girl-singer-lizzo-has-asthma-attack-on-stage-video.

Brown, A. M. (2019). *Pleasure activism: The politics of feeling good*. AK Press.

Cameron, N. O., Muldrow, A. F., & Stefani, W. (2018). The weight of things: Understanding African American women's perceptions of health, body image, and attractiveness. *Qualitative Health Research, 28*(8), 1242–1254. https://doi.org/10.1177/1049732317753588.

Cardena, C. (2019). A love letter to Lizzo: How the Houston-raised musician made a name for herself. *Texas Monthly*. https://www.texasmonthly.com/the-culture/how-lizzo-became-a-star-houston/.

CBS News This Morning. (2019). *Lizzo responds to criticism over revealing Lakers game outfit: "I stay in my own positive bubble."* https://www.cbsnews.com/video/lizzo-responds-to-criticism-over-revealing-lakers-game-outfit-i-stay-in-my-own-positive-bubble/?intcid=CNM-00-10abd1h.

CBS News This Morning. (2020). *How Lizzo went from "band nerd" to this year's most Grammy-nominated artist*. https://www.cbsnews.com/news/lizzo-on-her-success-how-she-got-her-name-her-depression-after-her-dad-died-and-her-love-of-classical-music/.

Centers for Disease Control and Prevention. (2018). *Health of Black or African American non-Hispanic population*. Retrieved November 2, 2020, from https://www.cdc.gov/nchs/fastats/black-health.htm.

Chavez, K. (2019, July 30). *The decade of Lizzo is just getting started*. Marie Claire. https://www.marieclaire.com/celebrity/a28542850/lizzo-abs olut-juice-interview/.

Chen, G., Williams, S., Hendrickson, N., & Chen, L. (2012). Male mammies: A social-comparison perspective on how exaggeratedly overweight media portrayals of Madea, Rasputia, and big momma affect how Black women feel about themselves. *Mass Communication & Society, 15*(1), 115–135. https://doi.org/10.1080/15205436.2011.569682.

Cohen, B. C. (1963). *The press and foreign policy*. Princeton, NJ: Princeton University Press.

Collins, Patricia Hill. (2004). *Black sexual politics*. New York: Routledge.

Conti, G. (2019, May 21). *I denied my eating disorder for years. This is why I'm finally talking about it*. Hello Giggles. https://hellogiggles.com/lifestyle/den ied-my-eating-disorder-for-years/.

Cooper, B. (2012, December 31). *(Un)Clutching my mother's pearls, or ratch-etness and the residue of respectability* [Blog post]. https://crunkfeministcolle

ctive.wordpress.com/2012/12/31/unclutching-mymothers-pearls-or-ratche tness-and-the-residue-of-respectability/.

Cottom, T. M. (2019). *Thick: and other essays*. The New Press.

Couch, D., Thomas, S. L., Lewis, S., Blood, R. W., & Komesaroff, P. (2015). Obese Adults' perceptions of news reporting on obesity: The panopticon and synopticon at Work. *SAGE Open, 5*(4), 1.

Couser, G. T. (2002). Signifying bodies: Life writing and disability studies. In S. L. Snyder, B. J. Brueggemann, & R. Garland-Thomson (Eds.), *Disability studies: Enabling the humanities* (pp. 109–117). New York: The Modern Language Association of America.

Coyne, S. M., Liechty, T., Collier, K. M., Sharp, A. D., Davis, E. J., & Kroff, S. L. (2018). The effect of media on body image in pregnant and postpartum women. *Health Communication, 33*(7), 793–799. https://doiorg.spot.lib.aub urn.edu/10.1080/10410236.2017.1314853.

Cruel, J. (2017). *Body-positive singer Lizzo doesn't care if you call her fat*. Self. https://www.self.com/story/lizzo-interview.

Daufin, E. K. (2020). Thick Sistahs and heavy disprivilege: Black women, inter-sectionality and weight stigma. In M. Friedman, C. Rice, & J. Rinaldi (Eds.), *Thickening fat: Fat bodies, intersectionality, and social justice* (pp. 160–170). Routledge.

Dent, G. (2019, July 13). Lizzo is a joyous inspiration—But body positivity has come too late for the likes of me. *The Guardian*.https://www.theguardian. com/commentisfree/2019/jul/13/grace-dent-lizzo-body-positivity-too-late-for-me.

D'Zurilla, C. (2017, March 8). Gabourey Sidibe on her dramatic weight loss: 'I did it so I can walk around comfortably in heels'. *Los Angeles Times*. https://www.latimes.com/entertainment/gossip/la-et-mg-gabourey-sidibe-weight-memoir-20170308-story.htm.

Edwards, E. B., & Esposito, J. (2018). Reading the black woman's body via instagram fame. *Communication, Culture and Critique, 11*(3), 341–358. https://doi.org/10.1093/ccc/tcy011.

Enjoli, A. (2020). *10 ways to practice self-love, according to Lizzo*. Live Kindly. https://www.livekindly.co/waitrose-uk-first-vegan-cheese-fondue/.

Entman, R. M. (1993). Framing: Toward clarification of a fractured paradigm. *Journal of Communication, 43*(4), 51–58. https://doi-org.spot.lib.auburn. edu/10.1111/j.1460-2466.1993.tb01304.x.

Feller, M. (2019, October 3). Hot girl summer is over: Fat bear fall is here. *Elle*. https://www.elle.com/culture/celebrities/a29350153/fat-bear-week-explained/.

Field, A. E., Cheung, L., Wolf, A. M., Herzog, D. B., Gortmaker, S. L., & Colditz, G. A. (1999). Exposure to the mass media and weight concerns among girls. *Pediatrics, 103*(3), 660.

Fikkan, J. L., & Rothblum, E. D. (2012). Is fat a feminist issue? Exploring the gendered nature of weight bias. *Sex Roles, 66*, 575–592. https://doi.org/10.1007/s11199-011-0022-5.

Flake, E. (2017, February 12). *As #BlackGirlMagic turns four years old, CaShawn Thompson has a fresh word for all the magical Black girls.* https://blavity.com/as-blackgirlmagic-turns-four-years-old-cashawnthompson-has-a-fresh-word-for-all-the-magical-black-girls.

Fontaine, S. (2010, April 5). Is "precious" star Gabby Sidibe too fat for a Hollywood career? *NewsOne.* https://newsone.com/478842/is-precious-star-gabby-sidibe-too-fat-for-a-hollywood-career/.

For Harriet. (2020, December 19). Yes, you're fatphobic. w/ Dr. Joy Cox and @AmaPoundcake [video]. For Harriet. YouTube. https://www.youtube.com/watch?v=R68B6QmXevY&feature=youtu.be.

France, W. (2019, September 5). *All the reasons why we love Lizzo.* The Nicholls Worth. https://thenichollsworth.com/7007586/showcase/all-the-reasons-why-we-love-lizzo/.

Gamboa, G. (2019, November 5). *Lizzo is primed to end cancel culture.* CNN. https://www.cnn.com/2019/11/05/opinions/lizzo-cancel-culture-opinion-gamboa/index.html.

Garcia, A. (2020, October 28). The Instagram nudity policy is changing to be more inclusive of plus-size bodies. *Glamour.* https://www.glamour.com/story/the-instagram-nudity-policy-is-changing-to-be-more-inclusive-of-plus-size-bodies.

Gardner, A. (2020). Lizzo wants the world to know being fat is normal. *Glamour.* https://www.glamour.com/story/lizzo-wants-the-world-to-know-being-fat-is-normal.

Garland-Thomson, R. (1997). *Extraordinary bodies: Figuring physical disability in American culture and literature.* New York: Columbia University Press.

Gay, R. (2017). *Hunger: A memoir of (my) body* (1st edn.). Harper, an imprint of Harper Collins Publishers.

Gentles-Peart, K. (2016). *Romance with voluptuousness: Caribbean women and thick bodies in the United States.* University of Nebraska Press.

George, J. A. (2015). Stereotype and school pushout: Race, gender, and discipline disparities in the context of school discipline disparities. *Arkansas Law Review, 68*(1), 101–129.

George, K. (2019, August 1). *Bad bitch.* Urban Dictionary. https://www.urbandictionary.com/define.php?term=A%20bad%20bitch.

Glenn, N. M., McGannon, K. R., & Spence, J. C. (2013). Exploring media representations of weight-loss surgery. *Qualitative Health Research, 23*(5), 631–644. https://doi-org.spot.lib.auburn.edu/10.1177/1049732471731.

Goffman, E. (1963). *Stigma: Notes on the management of a spoiled identity*. New York: Prentice-Hall.

Greenbaum-Davis, D. (2019, August 26). Lizzo and the politically incorrect obesity epidemic. *The Spectator*. https://spectator.us/lizzo-problem-plus-size-role-models/.

Gross, T. (2017, May 8). Actress Gabourey Sidibe on anxiety, phone sex and life after 'precious' [Audio podcast episode]. In *Fresh Air*. National Public Radio. https://www.npr.org/2017/05/08/527392123/actress-gabourey-sidibe-on-anxiety-phone-sex-and-life-after-precious.

Gross, T. (2019, May 23). Lizzo on feminism, self-love and bringing 'Hallelujah Moments' to stage [Audio podcast episode]. In *Fresh Air*. National Public Radio Online. https://www.npr.org/2019/05/23/725704911/lizzo-on-feminism-self-love-and-bringing-hallelujah-moments-to-stage.

Harris-Perry, M. (2016, April 26). A call and response with Melissa Harris-Perry: The pain and the power of lemonade. What happens when we take the hopes, dreams, pain, and joy of black girls and women and put them in the center? *Elle*. https://www.elle.com/culture/music/a35903/lemonade-call-and-response/.

Harvey, O. (2020, December 16). *Lizzo posted a self-love mantra clapping back at her Detox backlash*. Hello Giggles. https://hellogiggles.com/news/lizzo-defended-decision-to-detox/.

Haywood, C. A. (2013, April 23). *The cranky conservative* [Video]. YouTube. https://www.youtube.com/channel/UCMRJ_dU6I4LZipMV_OBkvPQ/about.

Haywood, C. A. (2019, August 26). *The Black hat/sisters, there's a difference between being 'thick' and being fat*. The Electronic Urban Report. https://eurweb.com/2019/08/26/the-black-hat-sisters-theres-a-difference-between-being-thick-and-being-fat/.

Hello Beautiful Staff. (2019, November 22). *9 Times Lizzo reminded us sexiness doesn't come in one size fits all*. Hello Beautiful. https://hellobeautiful.com/playlist/9-times-lizzo-reminded-us-sexiness-doesnt-come-in-one-size-fits-all/item/1.

Hello Beautiful Staff. (2020). *About us*. https://hellobeautiful.com/about-2/.

Higginbotham, E. B. (1993). *Righteous discontent: The women's movement in the Black Baptist church, 1880–1920*. Cambridge, MA: Harvard University Press.

HipHollywood. (2013, July 5). *Why Kelly price created new reality TV show 'too fat for fame'* [Video]. https://www.youtube.com/watch?v=6WBJYn7aE28.

Hofstetter, A. (2019, August 22). Lizzo, I'm crying Cuz I love you. *Washington Square News*. https://nyunews.com/2019/08/22/lizzo-fat-women-acceptability-cultural-transformation/.

Hughes, B. (2019, April 23). *Lizzo is singing the self-care message we all need to hear in 2019*. Parade. https://parade.com/873822/beckyhughes/lizzo-new-album-self-love-body-positivity/.

Hurtado, A. (2020, April 27). *32 Lizzo lyrics about self-love that will get you pumped to celebrate the singer's birthday!* Parade. https://parade.com/944081/alexandra-hurtado/lizzo-lyrics-self-love-quotes/.

Irby, S. (2019). *Lizzo: TIMES's entertainer of the year*. https://time.com/entertainer-of-the-year-2019-lizzo/.

Jasinski, J. (2001). The status of theory and method in rhetorical criticism. *Western Journal of Communication, 65*(3), 249–270.

Johnson, S. (2019, August 27). *Lizzo makes me proud to be a plus-size Black woman*. Metro, UK. https://metro.co.uk/2019/08/27/lizzo-makes-me-proud-to-be-a-plus-size-black-woman-10639521/.

Jones, D. (2019, July 21). *Megan Thee Stallion, Cardi B and Lizzo are leading a pleasure politics revolution*. NBC News. https://www.nbcnews.com/think/opinion/megan-thee-stallion-cardi-b-lizzo-are-leading-pleasure-politics-ncna1029961.

Kaye, B. (2019). Azealia Banks calls Lizzo "millennial mammy" in unprompted Instagram tirade. *Yahoo! Life*. https://www.yahoo.com/lifestyle/azealia-banks-calls-lizzo-millennial-215020064.html.

Kirven, J. (2019, August 9). *Fat is not fab*. QNotes. https://goqnotes.com/63555/fat-is-not-fab/.

Kothesakis, E. (2019, September 17). Self-love and a flute: How Lizzo rose to fame. *The Hofstra Chronicle*. https://www.thehofstrachronicle.com/category/arts-and-entertainment/2019/9/16/self-love-and-a-flute-how-lizzo-rose-to-fame.

Kulbaga, T., & Spencer, L. (2018). Fitness and the feminist first lady: Gender, race, and body in Michelle Obama's let's move! Campaign. *Women and Language, 40*, 1.

Kurutz, S. (2018, September 13). Rihanna talks Lingerie, body positivity and her 'battle' with social media. *The New York Times*. https://www.nytimes.com/2018/09/13/fashion/rihanna-fenty-savage-new-york-fashion-week.html.

LaVoulle, C., & Lewis Ellison, T. (2018). The bad bitch Barbie Craze and Beyoncé African American Women's bodies as commodities in Hip-Hop culture, images, and media. *Taboo: The Journal of Culture and Education, 16*, 2. https://doi.org/10.31390/taboo.16.2.07.

Laymon, K. (2018). *Heavy: An American memoir*. Scribner.

LeBesco, K. (2004). *Revolting bodies? The struggle to redefine fat identity*. Amherst and Boston: University of Massachusetts Press.

Levine, N. (2019, December 27). *Why Lizzo was the star who defined 2019*. BBC. https://www.bbc.com/culture/article/20191218-why-lizzo-was-the-star-who-defined-2019.

Lizzo [@lizzobeeating]. (2019, April 1–November 30). *Official Instagram for Lizzo*. https://www.instagram.com/lizzobeeating/.

Lizzo [@Lizzo]. (2020, December 9). *Post* [Official TikTok for Lizzo]. Retrieved from https://www.tiktok.com/@lizzo/video/6904153428281396486?lang=en.

Lopez, J. (2019). Truth Hurts' was a viral hit, but Lizzo's Stardom is no accident. *Billboard*. https://www.billboard.com/articles/news/8530113/lizzo-billboard-cover-story-interview/.

Lundy, A. (2018). Caught between a Thot and a hard place: The politics of Black Female sexuality at the intersection of cinema and reality television. *The Black Scholar, 48*(1), 56–70. https://doi.org/10.1080/00064246.2018.1402256.

Lupton, D. (2017). Digital media and body weight, shape, and size: An introduction and review. *Fat Studies, 6*(2), 119–134.

MacMillan, A. (2017). Why Instagram is the worst social media for mental health. *Time*. https://time.com/4793331/instagram-social-media-mental-health/.

McCombs, M., Ghanem, S. I., Reese, S. D., Gandy, J. O. H., & Grant, A. E. (2001). The convergence of agenda setting and framing. In *Framing public life: Perspectives on media & our understanding of the social world* (pp. 67–82).

McKee, A. (2001) A beginner's guide to textual analysis. *Metro Magazine*, pp. 138–149.

McKee, A. (2003). *Textual analysis: A beginner's guide*. Sage Publications.

Mitchell, A., & Herring, K. (1998). *What the blues is all about: Black women overcoming stress and depression*. New York: Perigee.

Morris, C. E., & Sloop, J. M. (2006). What lips these lips have kissed: Refiguring the politics of queer public kissing. *Communication and Critical/Cultural Studies, 3*(1), 1–26.

Moulton, N. (2019, July 17). *Why it's time for big beauty brands to embrace body positivity*. Vogue Australia. https://www.vogue.com.au/beauty/news/why-its-time-for-big-beauty-brands-to-embrace-body-positivity/image-gallery/fcd f81f04120e099616b323a2012871e.

Murphy, D. (2019). *Lizzo opens up about her dating life and getting hit on after the MTV VMAs (Exclusive)*. Entertainment Tonight. https://www.etonline.com/lizzo-opens-up-about-her-dating-life-and-getting-hit-on-after-the-mtv-vmas-exclusive-131356.

Murrell, M. (2019, August 28). *Lizzo isn't here for your backward compliments when it comes to her body*. Buzzfeed. https://www.buzzfeed.com/morganmur rell/lizzo-brave-wrong-word-for-self-love.

Nicholas-Williams, N. [@curvynyome]. (2020a, August 14). *Post* [Instagram]. https://www.instagram.com/p/CD4JD6GAEdi/?utm_source=ig_embed.

Nicholas-Williams, N. [@curvynyome]. (2020b, September 10). *Post* [Instagram]. https://www.instagram.com/p/CE89AYDAMRy/?utm_source=ig_web_copy_link.

Nieves, B. (2019, September 4). How to dress like Lizzo this fall 2019. *Teen Vogue*. https://www.teenvogue.com/story/dress-like-lizzo.

Nnadi, C. (2018, May 3). *Rihanna on body image, turning 30, and staying real—No matter what*. https://www.vogue.com/article/rihanna-vogue-cover-june-issue-2018.

Page Six Team. (1999, November 30). 50 Fat Celebrities. *Page Six*. https://pagesix.com/1999/11/30/50-fat-celebrities/#1.

Parasecoli, F. (2007). Bootylicious: Food and the female body in contemporary Black Pop Culture. *Women's Studies Quarterly, 35*(1/2), 110–125. http://www.jstor.org/stable/27649657.

Patterson-Faye, C. J. (2016). 'I like the way you move': Theorizing fat, black and sexy. *Sexualities, 19*(8), 926–944. https://doi.org/10.1177/1363460716640731.

Perelman, C., & Olbrechts-Tyteca, L. (1969). *The new rhetoric: A treatise on argumentation*. Notre Dame, IN: University of Notre Dame Press.

Pickens, T. A. (2015). Shoving aside the politics of respectability: Black women, reality TV, and the ratchet performance. *Women and Performance: A Journal of Feminist Theory, 25*(1), 41–58.

Pickett Miller, N. (2019). "Other" White storytellers: Emancipating Albinism Identity through Personal Narratives. *Communication Quarterly, 67*(2), 123–139.

Price, J. (2019). Azealia banks thinks Lizzo is 'Making a Fool of Herself for a White American Public. *Complex Media*. https://www.complex.com/music/2019/09/azealia-banks-lizzo-making-fool-of-herself-white-american-public.

Ravary, A., Bartz, J. A., & Baldwin, M. W. (2019). Shaping the body politic: Mass media fat-shaming affects implicit anti-fat attitudes. *Personality & Social Psychology Bulletin, 11*, 1580.

Recording Academy Grammy Awards. (2020). *Grammy award results for Lizzo*. https://www.grammy.com/grammys/artists/lizzo.

Respers-France, L. (2019, July 31). *Lizzo and the dichotomy of big girl praise*. CNN. https://www.cnn.com/2019/07/31/entertainment/lizzo-plus-size-analysis/index.html.

Richards, A. (2016, January 17). *15 Times Queen Latifah was a + size fashion icon*. Bustle. https://www.bustle.com/articles/135627-15-times-queen-latifah-was-the-plus-size-fashion-icon-of-your-dreams-photos.

Richardson, D. (2019, April 10). What Lizzo means to me as a fat Black Girl. *Evolve Magazine*.https://www.evolvemagazine.online/current/what-lizzo-means-to-me-as-a-fat-black-girl.

Rivero, A. (2019, October 30). Opinion: Why Lizzo did what Meghan Trainor couldn't. *The Student Life.* https://tsl.news/opinion-why-lizzo-did-what-meg han-trainor-couldnt/.

Rhodes, B. (2019). Azealia Banks savagely attacks Lizzo on Instagram in barrage of name calling. *The Grio.* https://thegrio.com/2019/09/05/azealia-banks-savagely-attacks-lizzo-on-instagram-in-barrage-of-name-calling/.

Roberts, A., & Muta, S. (2017). Representations of female body weight in the media: An update of Playboy magazine from 2000 to 2014. *Body Image, 20,* 16–19. https://doi-org.spot.lib.auburn.edu/10.1016/j.bodyim. 2016.08.009.

Rodden, J. (2008). How do stories convince us? Notes towards a rhetoric of narrative. *College Literature, 35*(1), 148–173.

Ruiz de Castilla, C. (2017). Close reading. In M. Allen (Ed.), *The sage encyclopedia of communication research methods* (Vol. 1, pp. 137–139). Sage. https://www.doi.org/10.4135/9781483381411.n58.

Saguy, A. C., & Ward, A. (2011). Coming out as fat: Rethinking Stigma. *Social Psychology Quarterly, 74,* 53–75.

Savin, J. (2020, August 24). Instagram makes changes to stop censoring plus size Black women. *Yahoo! Sports.* https://sports.yahoo.com/instagram-makes-cha nges-stop-censoring-162600409.html.

Schalk, S. (2019, October 18). *When I twerked onstage with Lizzo, it was an act of political defiance.* Vox. https://www.vox.com/first-person/2019/10/18/ 20920615/twerking-with-lizzo.

Schallon, L. (2019, August 26). The fashion industry has a plus-size problem. These women want to fix it. *Glamour.* https://www.glamour.com/story/ what-its-like-to-be-plus-size-and-work-in-fashion.

Scheufele, D. A., & Tewksbury, D. (2007). Framing, agenda setting, and priming: The evolution of three media effects models. *Journal of Communication, 57*(1), 9–20. https://doi-org.spot.lib.auburn.edu/10.1111/j.0021-9916.2007.00326.x.

Seemayer, Z. (2015, July 29). *Raven-Symone says she was fat-shamed as a 7-year-old.* Entertainment Tonight. https://www.etonline.com/news/168972_ raven_symone_says_she_was_fat_shamed_as_a_7_year_old.

Senyonga, M. (2017). Microaggressions, marginality, and mediation at the intersections: Experiences of Black fat women in academia. *Inter Actions: UCLA Journal of Education & Information Studies, 13*(1), 1–23.

Shafer, E. (2019, June 26). *Here are the lyrics to Lizzo's 'truth hurts'.* Billboard. https://www.billboard.com/articles/news/lyrics/8517815/lizzo-truth-hurts-lyrics.

Sheldon, P., & Wiegand, A. (2019). "Am I as pretty and smart as she is?" Competition for attention and social comparison on Instagram. *Carolinas Communication Annual, 35,* 63–75.

Shiffer, E. (2019, October 28). *Lizzo just posted a nude Instagram lying in a skittles-filled bathtub, and it's everything.* Women's Health. https://www.wom enshealthmag.com/life/a29610302/lizzo-nude-instagram-nsfw-bathtub-ski ttles/.

Shropshire, T. (2011, May 11). *Jill Scott loses 50 pounds, but does she look better? Rolling out.* https://rollingout.com/2011/05/12/jill-scott-loses-50-pounds-but-does-she-look-better/.

Silverstein, B., Perdue, L., Peterson, B., & Kelly, E. (1986). The role of the mass media in promoting a thin standard of bodily attractiveness for women. *Sex Roles, 14*(9–10), 519.

Smith, S., Della, L., Rajack-Talley, T., D'Silva, M., Potter, D., Markowitz, L., Craig, L., Cheatham, K., & Carthan, Q. (2013). Exploring media's impact on African American women's healthy food habits in Kentucky. *Journal of Intercultural Communication Research, 42*(3), 228–251. https://doi.org/10. 1080/17475759.2013.823455.

Snider, I. N. (2018). Girl bye: Turning from stereotypes to self-defined Images, a womanist exploration on representation and crooked room theory. *Kaleidoscope: A Graduate Journal of Qualitative Communication, 17*, 11–20.

Southard-Ospina, M. (2019, July 3). *Why Miley Cyrus' 'mother's daughter' video matters in our fat-shaming society.* Bustle. https://www.bustle.com/p/why-miley-cyrus-mothers-daughter-video-matters-in-our-fat-shaming-culture-181 68565.

Stallings, L. H. (2013). Hip hop and the Black ratchet imagination. *Palimpsest: A Journal on Women, Gender, and the Black International, 2*(2), 135–139.

Stephens, B. (2019, August 23). *Blame it on her juice: Over 60 of Lizzo's sexiest photos.* Pop Sugar UK. https://www.popsugar.co.uk/celebrity/Sexy-Lizzo-Pictures-46537803.

Strings, S. (2015). Obese Black Women as "social dead weight": Reinventing the "diseased Black Woman." *Signs, 41*(1), 107–130. https://doi-org.spot. lib.auburn.edu/10.1086/681773.

Strings, S. (2019). *Fearing the black body: The racial origins of fat phobia.* New York University Press.

Sullivan, C. (2019, September 24). Lizzo's song lyrics about love will make you feel 100% that b*tch. *Elite Daily.* https://www.elitedaily.com/p/lizzos-song-lyrics-about-love-will-make-you-feel-100-that-btch-18792100.

Sydneysky G. (2019). Unraveling the fatphobia behind the criticism of Lizzo. https://wearyourvoicemag.com/unraveling-the-fatphobia-behind-the-criticisms-of-lizzo/.

Tankovska, H. (2020). *Instagram - statistics & facts.* Retrieved from https:// www.statista.com/topics/1882/instagram/.

The Core 94! Radio Station. (2020, April 21). Quarantine Chronicles Ep. 4—Kelly Price part 2 [Video]. YouTube. https://www.youtube.com/watch?v=G4Gi3c0aYOo&t=15s.

The Mammy Caricature. (2020). *Ferris State University Jim Crow Museum of Racist Memorabilia*. https://www.ferris.edu/jimcrow/mammies/.

The View. (2019, August 1). Jerry O'Connell talks Mariah Carey and 'real housewives' [Video].YouTube. https://youtu.be/iiAavFGPdpE.

Toliver, S. R. (2019). Breaking Binaries: #BlackGirlMagic and the Black Ratchet imagination. *Journal of Language and Literacy Education, 15*, 1.

Torres, K. (2019, November 22). *Lizzo—Queen of body positivity—Just shared a pic of her butt along with a hilarious photoshop.* Buzzfeed. https://www.buzzfeed.com/kristatorres/lizzo-queen-of-body-positivity-just-shared-a-pic-of-her.

Trammell, K. (2019, April 2). *Lizzo is the musical artist you need to hear right now.* WVTA News. https://www.wtva.com/content/national/508879932.html.

Tsjeng, Z. (2019, November 9). Lizzo: "I'm not trying to sell you me. I'm trying to sell you, you". *Vogue UK.* https://www.vogue.co.uk/news/article/lizzo-british-vogue-interview.

Tyree, T. C. M., Byerly, C. M., & Hamilton, K.-A. (2012). Representations of (new) Black masculinity: A news-making case study. *Journalism: Theory, Practice, and Criticism, 13*(4), 467–482. https://doi-org.spot.lib.auburn.edu/10.1177/1464884911421695.

Unbothered [@r29unbothered]. (2020, January 16). Go Off Sis S2 Ep. 11 [post]. Instagram. https://www.instagram.com/tv/B7Y3zXynZlY/?utm_source=ig_web_copy_link.

U.S. Department of Health and Human Services Office of Minority Health. (2020). *Obesity and African Americans.* Retrieved December 18, 2020, from https://minorityhealth.hhs.gov/omh/browse.aspx?lvl=4&lvlid=25.

Uwumarogie, V. (2016, December 1). Kelly Price shows off new slim, trimmed figure. *MadameNoire.* https://madamenoire.com/727909/kelly-price-weight-loss/.

Van Gelder, T. (2005). Teaching critical thinking: Some lessons from cognitive science. *College Teaching, 53*(1), 41–46.

Vega, I., & Miller, R. (2019). Pop culture deserves academic recognition. *The Signal.* https://tcnjsignal.net/2019/02/26/pop-culture-deserves-academic-recognition/.

Vogue (2019). Met gala 2019 Red Carpet: See all the celebrity dresses, outfits, and looks here. https://www.vogue.com/slideshow/met-gala-2019-red-carpet-livecelebrity-fashion.

Weaver, D. H. (2007). Thoughts on agenda setting, framing, and priming. *Journal of Communication, 57*(1), 142–147. https://doi-org.spot.lib.auburn.edu/10.1111/j.1460-2466.2006.00333.x.

Weidhase, N. (2015). 'Beyoncé feminism' and the contestation of the black feminist body. *Celebrity Studies, 6*(1), 128–131. https://doi.org/10.1080/19392397.2015.1005389.

Weiner, J. (2019, August 16). The abrupt end of my big girl summer. *The New York Times*. https://www.nytimes.com/2019/08/16/opinion/lizzo-kelly-mcgillis.html.

Weinstock, S. (2019, April 3). Fat People Fuck Too. *DigBoston*. https://digboston.com/fat-people-fuck-too/.

Wells, V. (2019, April 5). Lizzo recounts a boyfriend telling her body needed work & getting to self-acceptance. *MadameNoire*. https://madamenoire.com/1068194/lizzo-boyfriend-body-shaming/.

Whitfield, K. (2018, October 12). *Fat, Black women's bodies are under attack. Why did it take a thin White man to get our cries heard?* Rewire News Group. https://rewirenewsgroup.com/article/2018/10/12/fat-black-womens-bodies-are-under-attack-why-did-it-take-a-thin-white-man-to-get-our-cries-heard/.

Willett, C. [@clairewillett]. (2018, November 3). [Tweet]. https://twitter.com/clairewillett/status/1058604984311341056.

Yioutas, J., & Segvic, I. (2003). Revisiting the Clinton/Lewinsky scandal: The convergence of agenda setting and framing. *Journalism & Mass Communication Quarterly, 3*, 567.

Zhang, Y., Dixon, T. L., & Conrad, K. (2009). Rap music videos and African American Women's body image: The moderating role of ethnic identity. *Journal of Communication, 59*(2), 262–278. https://doi.org/10.1111/j.1460-2466.2009.01415.x.

INDEX

CPSIA information can be obtained
at www.ICGtesting.com
Printed in the USA
LVHW082048060922
727576LV00030B/441

9 783030 737610